THE
WORKING
OF
MIRACLES

AND OTHER PROPHETIC WRITINGS

THE
WORKING
OF
MIRACLES

AND OTHER PROPHETIC WRITINGS

3-BOOKS-IN-1

H. A. MAXWELL
WHYTE

W

WHITAKER
HOUSE

This book is not intended to provide medical advice or to take the place of medical advice and treatment from your personal physician. Readers are advised to consult their own doctors or other qualified health professionals regarding the treatment of their medical problems. Neither the publisher nor the author takes any responsibility for any possible consequences from any treatment, action, or application of medicine, supplement, herb, or preparation to any person reading or following the information in this book. If readers are taking prescription medications, they should consult with their physicians and not take themselves off medicines to start supplementation without the proper supervision of a physician.

THE WORKING OF MIRACLES AND OTHER PROPHETIC WRITINGS

Includes the following books:
The Working of Miracles
The Prophetic Word
Pulling Down Strongholds

ISBN: 978-1-64123-229-6
eBook ISBN: 978-1-64123-230-2
Printed in the United States of America
© 2019 by Michael Whyte

Whitaker House
1030 Hunt Valley Circle
New Kensington, PA 15068
www.whitakerhouse.com

Library of Congress Cataloging-in-Publication Data (Pending)

1 2 3 4 5 6 7 8 9 10 11 ⨄ 26 25 24 23 22 21 20 19

CONTENTS

THE WORKING OF MIRACLES

CONTENTS

But the manifestation of the Spirit is given to each one for the profit of all…. To another [is given] the working of miracles.
—1 Corinthians 12:7, 10

INTRODUCTION

In the last few years, there has been an outpouring of the Holy Spirit unequalled since the days of the early church. This new visitation to the church, in its largest sense, has seen a return of the charismatic gifts of the Spirit, spelled out in the twelfth chapter of 1 Corinthians, including the one called *"the working of miracles"* (1 Corinthians 12:10). The ability to work miracles is given to some in the church. It is not hard to understand the basic meaning of the English words, for in *The Living Bible*, we read *"He gives power for doing miracles to some."*

This is a big departure from the old approach in prayer, in which petitions were made to God through Jesus Christ, for these prayers do not fulfill the primary requirements contained in 1 Corinthians 12:10. Here we understand that certain Spiritfilled persons will actually expedite a miracle by *doing it*. Once this fact has been realized and one has developed the faith and the ability to work miracles, then these will occur, depending on the faith of the one desiring the miracle.

This book unfolds the principles involved in the working of miracles and the explanation of what a miracle really is. Some are still saying that the day of miracles is past, but they are not up to date or with the times, for the days of miracles are very much with us today.

1

EVANGELISM BY MIRACLES

Many believed in His name when they saw the signs which He did.
—John 2:23

The world is beginning to witness the greatest outpouring of the Holy Spirit since the days of the apostles of the early church. The only answer to the mounting problems of the world is a fresh revelation of God and His Son, Jesus. The expression "renewal of the church" is being heard on every side today, but to some this means "renewal of my denomination," and there has been a tendency for charismatic groups to gather within the confines of their old-line denominations and try to corral the Holy Spirit in their group. God will not revive sectarianism, but will destroy it by the brightness of His splendor. It is written in Revelation 21:5 that, in the end time, *"Behold, I make all things new."* The renewal of the church by Jesus Christ, through a renewal of the Holy Spirit, will not only completely change the present structures of denominations, but will bring back one true church in which the working of miracles will be the norm. These abundant miracles will be recognized by denominational leaders, who will then have to make a decision: align with Jesus or attempt to bolster the old, crumbling walls. They will discover that their roof will collapse as the new wind of the Spirit blows through their church.

The religious leaders of the state religion of Israel created a council to discuss the embarrassment caused by Jesus coming among them with miracles. *"Then the chief priests and the Pharisees gathered a council and said, "What shall we do? [or, What shall we do?] For this Man works many signs* [miracles]. *If we let Him alone like this, everyone will believe in Him"* (John 11:47–48). Their anxiety was not spiritual but political, for they feared that the Romans would take away their authority and recognize the spiritual authority of Jesus, and that, as a result, they would lose many followers. This is the spirit of denominationalism—and it *is* a spirit. They were more interested in status, property, salaries, and the opinion of the masses than in seeing the Jewish "church" renewed.

Let us focus on the fact that the methods Jesus used were essentially miraculous. Jesus never held a workshop on evangelism. He never taught people how to "save souls." No spiritual laws were given to His disciples. His method was simple—do miracles! Then, *when* the people saw the miracles He did, many believed in Him. The priests did not deny that a large number of unexplainable miracles had been done. They feared them. They knew that these supernatural signs would cause the people to believe to claim that Jesus was their Messiah. This was the last thing that the temple leaders wanted to happen. They knew perfectly well what Jesus thought about them—*"scribes and Pharisees, hypocrites!"* (Matthew 23:13). They not only prevented others from accessing the kingdom of God, but they themselves refused to participate.

If the Jewish leaders had believed in Him and welcomed Him as the sent one of God and the deliverer of Israel, the whole of the Jewish organization could have moved forward to the next step—spiritual renewal. All the Jewish people could have moved toward the Day of Pentecost, which was a Jewish feast day. Instead of there being only one hundred twenty in the upper room, there could have been hundreds of thousands upon whom the tongues of fire would have rested. The wind of the Spirit would have blown throughout the streets of Jerusalem, and thousands upon thousands would have begun to speak in other tongues as the Spirit gave them the utterance. (See Acts 2:1–4.) This was the crucial day of renewal, and the "church," as it existed then, failed, but a remnant succeeded. In fact, by the end of the first week after Pentecost, the score stood at 8,120 believing Jews—renewed in the Holy Spirit, manifesting the charismatic gifts of the Spirit. Many of the Jewish leaders explained away this renewal by stating that these were drunk at nine o'clock in the morning! (See Acts 2:15.)

There was no such thing as "charismatic Pharisees" or "charismatic Sadducees," for on the Day of Pentecost, the true church came into existence, which is the body of Christ. Always remember that a Jewish person who accepts Jesus as the Messiah, and who is baptized in the Holy Spirit as on the Day of Pentecost, becomes a "completed Jew," ready to explore the mysteries of Jehovah's kingdom. All the original apostles of the Lamb were Jewish, and Paul, the first apostle of the church, and was also Jewish.

TODAY, WE ARE WITNESSING THE HOLY SPIRIT RAISING UP NEW LEADERSHIP AMONG THE GENTILES. THERE WILL BE MODERN APOSTLES AND PROPHETS, BUT THE SAME HALLMARK WILL BE UPON THEM—THEY WILL BE WORKERS OF MIRACLES.

Today, we are witnessing the Holy Spirit raising up new leadership among the Gentiles. There will be modern apostles and prophets, but the same hallmark will be upon them—they will be workers of miracles. This will be their spiritual seal of office. *"And Stephen, full of faith and* power, did great wonders and signs among the people" (Acts 6:8). Instead of rejoicing that the power of God was revealed through a humble servant of God, they stoned Stephen to death, just as they killed the Son of God.

In Acts 4:16, the Jewish church leaders did not try to hide the fact that a miracle had occurred; in fact, they referred to it as a "*notable miracle*." Peter and John were apostles of the Lord and had been used as instruments to heal a lame man at the gate Beautiful.

> *And seeing the man who had been healed standing with them, they could say nothing against it* [the miracle]. *But when they had commanded them to go aside out of the council, they conferred among themselves, saying, "What shall we do to these men? For, indeed, that a notable miracle has been done through them is evident to all who dwell in Jerusalem, and we cannot deny it.*   (Acts 4:14–16)

Their only answer was to threaten the apostles Peter and John and forbid them to speak about Jesus, who was risen from the dead. (See Acts 4:2, 18.) Of course, the apostles refused this ungodly council from the recognized religious rulers of the Jews.

Do we not see a parallel today among some denominational leaders? Others, however, are beginning to see and believe because of the miracles.

What is a *miracle?* Today, the word is usually applied to drugs or food stores. If a new drug cures a stubborn sickness, it is called a "miracle drug"! When prayer brings healing in a person with cancer, they say "it has gone into remission." These are the acrobatic contortions people of unbelief will perform to deny the miracle. The media will widely publish a new miracle drug but suppress accounts of true miracles of healing and deliverance.

A miracle is an act of the power of God that transcends human ability or understanding. There are two words in the Greek: one is *dunamis*, which simply means "power," and the other is *semeion*, which means "a sign given supernaturally." Thus, the charismatic gifts of 1 Corinthians 12 are often referred to as "sign gifts." The original speaking in tongues on the Day of Pentecost was a sign gift from heaven—a supernatural sign that the Jewish leaders failed to understand. Speaking in tongues is always miraculous. The healing of the sick, or the deliverance of those whom Satan has bound, are powerful manifestations of *dunamis*. Jesus used this word when He promised, *"But you shall receive **power** [duna-mis] when the [at the same time] the Holy Spirit has come upon you"* (Acts 1:8). The word is used again when Jesus healed the woman suffering from hemorrhage. After she touched the hem of Jesus's garment, He felt power (*dunamis*) go out of Him. (See Mark 5:30.)

It can be readily seen that when we are baptized in the Holy Spirit, as at Pentecost, we receive power (*dunamis*) as the normal manifestation of the indwelling Spirit. Thus, one of the nine charismatic manifestations of the Spirit is *"the working of miracles"* (1 Corinthians 12:10). This spiritual enablement is for all believers who submit themselves to Jesus to receive the baptism in the Spirit. It is good to remember that in the great revival under John the Baptist, he promised that all who repented of their sins and submitted themselves to water baptism would receive the baptism of the Holy Spirit and fire. (See Mark 1:8.) Thus, the Jewish church was intended to participate in Pentecost after having seen the miracles that Jesus did on earth.

There are two types of miracles, therefore. One is a sign gift, such as speaking in tongues, interpretation of tongues, prophecy, the word of knowledge, or wisdom. Paul himself said that the speaking in tongues was a sign (*semeion*) to the unbeliever. (See 1 Corinthians 14:22.) He used the same word translated as "miracle." Thus, when we speak in tongues in the presence of an unbeliever, we actually manifest a sign miracle. Tongues will not be understood by unbelievers, but it will have a shattering effect on them, and they will have to make a decision one way or the other, either for the full gospel or for no gospel—or possibly for a limited, emasculated gospel, as taught in some denominations.

The other type of miracle is the power type. Jesus used both. To the woman at the well, He used a word of knowledge that caused her to say, "*Come, see a Man who told me all things that I ever did. Could this be the Christ?*" (John 4:29). This was a *semeion* miracle, which caused her to recognize that He was indeed the Christ. At other times, He opened blind eyes, unstopped deaf ears, raised the dead, healed bent spines, and restored people to health. These were the *dunamis* miracles. The clergy resisted Him at every step, but the common people sought Him eagerly. (See Mark 12:37.) They had everything to gain. The clergy could not do these things, and thus, they hated this Jesus who *did* work miracles.

The great restoration of the church is upon us. This renewing will be done solely by preaching the gospel, followed by a mass demonstration of miracles. Gimmicks, church entertainment, and wayout stunts will disappear. We shall not even need "magicians" to entertain the children. God will bare His holy arm as the Word sounds forth—for it is written, "*And they went out and preached everywhere, the Lord working with them and confirming the word through the accompanying signs [semeion]*" (Mark 16:20). We shall fulfill the commission as given in Matthew 10:8: "*Heal the sick, cleanse the lepers, raise the dead, cast out demons.*" We shall stick to this divine commission. We shall not vary from it. We shall not substitute anything else for it. It is the heart of the gospel. We shall not flinch when angry church-going people tell us that Christians cannot "have demons," or when they insist that the true gospel is a social gospel only. We shall adhere to the divine remedy for all mankind. We shall work miracles in His wonderful, holy name, and the people will hear us gladly, and multitudes will believe.

It all has to happen before Jesus comes.

2

LEG LENGTHENING

And behold, there was a woman who had
a spirit of infirmity eighteen years.
—Luke 13:11

The progressive outpouring of the Holy Spirit on the church has been gradual since the Reformation began in 1517. A greater move occurred at the beginning of the century by a reappearance of the sign miracle of speaking in tongues. In recent times, the effects of this new visitation have become very apparent in the charismatic renewal of the church. This renewal is a deeper move of the Spirit of God to bring people into a deeper knowledge of the Son of God, both experimentally and doctrinally, and also to demonstrate greater degrees of the miraculous.

An alert, praying Christian today will not be taken by surprise at greater revelations of the Spirit, but he will actually premeditate them and watch for them. We must ever keep in mind the words of Jesus: *"He who believes in Me, the works that I do he will do also; and greater works than these he will do"* (John 14:12). This promise has been in the Bible a long time, but it still shocks the institutionalized church and those who have taken an unrealistic dispensational stand. Greater works are for today.

It was in the late sixties that I began to hear about the phenomenon of "leg lengthening." My good friend Rev. Richard Vineyard was lengthening legs in Toronto, Ontario, at Evangel Temple. The reports stated that miracles were taking place there. This was a little too much for me but I went along to see. Unfortunately, it was impossible to see what was happening on the platform from the midst of the large congregation. We were informed from stage that "legs were growing." Frankly, I was not impressed. I could not see any evidence. I largely dismissed the matter from my mind as just another gimmick.

In 1971, I visited Huntington Beach, California, and was ministering healing and deliverance to about two hundred people. I came face to face with a man who told me he had a completely locked spine. Although he could stand up straight, he could not bend and had not touched his toes in twenty years. As I stood before him, the Lord brought to my remembrance the story of the woman who had double curvature of the spine. The Bible says she was bowed together and could in no way lift herself up. (See Luke 13:10–17.) I explained that this man's trouble was probably identical to this woman's malady. I said that I was going to rebuke the binding spirit of infirmity, and afterward, he would be able to bend his back. To this he readily agreed. I laid my hands on his head and roundly rebuked the spirit in Jesus's name, and then I commanded him to begin bending. It took eight minutes, and then he began shouting the praises of God. He could touch his toes for the first time in twenty years! This miracle did a great deal for my ministry; for one thing, it showed me that Richard Vineyard had probably been right, and I had been showing ignorant prejudice when confronted by a "greater work." How easy is this for the ministry!

The next shock came to me when visiting in Pompano Beach, Florida. I had been staying with Rev. Don Basham and we went to a local house group. After ministering healing and the gifts of the Spirit, a young man approached me, saying, "The Lord has revealed to me that you have one leg shorter than the other." This was indeed news to me, for I had lived with my legs all my life and was quite unaware that there was anything wrong with them! Of course, it must be admitted that I had never measured them! We usually don't behave like that, do we? The young man almost commanded me to sit down, and so I went along with this enthusiastic fanatic and sat down. He then told me to stretch my legs out and he held the heels in his hands. Straightway, he said, "Yes, your left leg is shorter than your right by a quarter of an inch!" By this time, I could do nothing. I was powerless! He was holding on to my feet! He prayed a short prayer and then exclaimed that God had done the miracle and my legs were now the same length. My reaction was of benign unbelief, for I couldn't I see a thing, and I felt nothing. I just had to thank him rather sheepishly and try to forget the whole embarrassing experience.

For as long as I can remember, whenever I had a suit made by my tailor, I had to emphasize that my right arm was half-an-inch shorter than the left. The tailor had to be careful, for on one occasion, he reversed the order; he misread the instructions on the order sheet. I had about six jackets, all of which had the right arm sleeve cut half-an-inch shorter. It was while preaching in my church in Toronto, a few weeks after this embarrassing experience, that my right sleeve kept riding way up my arm. I kept pulling it down, and then it rode up again. Next week, I had a change of suits, but the same thing happened. By this time, I was becoming distinctly suspicious that something had happened to my arm length. I didn't say a word to anyone, not even my wife. I returned to my tailor and asked him to measure my arms. He reported they were exactly the same length, so I asked him to alter the sleeve length of these two suit jackets. When I called for them, I took all my others along and asked him to alter them too, which he did—without comment or question. After all, let's face it, if I could not easily accept this kind of miracle, I could hardly expect my tailor to start asking me difficult questions!

I suddenly began to realize what had happened. When this young man prayed for my leg lengthening, the hand of Jesus had actually straightened my entire spinal column, and thereby, the shoulders were adjusted and my arms came out even! I must say, I was awed and told our congregation, who praised God and rejoiced. It seemed they had more faith for the miraculous than their pastor did!

It was a full year and a half later that I attended a conference of ministers at St. Louis, Missouri, in the summer of 1973. Among the ministers present was my friend Rev. Derek Prince. In his typical way, he nonchalantly offered to pray for anyone who might have a short leg. Several ministers volunteered for the experiment, and Derek held their ankles and prayed a simple prayer of faith. Before my eyes, I saw legs growing! Was I dreaming? I had never seen anything like this before. It was real! I was stunned! Richard Vineyard had been right after all, for he told me some years later in Baton Rouge, Louisiana, that the Lord had actually revealed to him that He would do this miracle on people if Richard would pray—so he began to pray!

Naturally the ministers began asking Derek Prince about this strange happening. He stated quite simply that it came under the heading of the *"working of miracles"* (1 Corinthians 12:10).

On returning home to my church, I felt I was riding on air. I had seen a visible miracle. Could I dare try? If so, who should I ask first? Obviously, the members of my own family. I was not aware that any of them had "short legs," for none limped, but at least if I made a fool of myself before them, they would forgive me! I wasn't so sure about the church, though! I finally asked my son Stephen, who was my assistant pastor. Sure enough, one of his legs was shorter, and when I prayed, it lengthened before my eyes! Stephen's wife, Gail, then approached a woman of the church, and, to her astonishment, she saw a leg grow as she prayed and watched. So this miracle could work for anyone, providing we prayed and believed.

Anyone who has been used of God to pray for this miracle and has seen it will never be quite the same again. It opens tremendous possibilities for miracles in minds and bodies, just by the laying on of hands and the simple prayer of faith. Knowing nothing about the chiropractic profession, the Holy Spirit began to teach us many things by revelation. He showed us that as the central nervous system runs through the middle of the spinal column, from the brain to all parts of the body, even to the soles of the feet, then any kink in the spine caused by worn or misplaced vertebrae would bring pressure on this nervous system and produce pains in various parts of the body. Some of these pains would be constant and stubborn, in the neck, back of the head, shoulders, arms, thighs, legs, and feet. I myself found that after my own leg miracle, all dull pains ceased in the right thigh, which used to be made manifest when I drove the car any distance. I even discovered that apparent allergies could be caused by this, as well as migraines and similar distressing pains. No wonder the Word of God told us that Jesus bore our pains.

*Surely He has borne our griefs and carried our **sorrows**; yet we esteemed Him stricken, smitten by God, and afflicted.*   (Isaiah 53:4)

In Isaiah 53:4, the word *"sorrows"* is from the Hebrew *makob*, which means "pains." How many pains can be caused by a spinal column being distorted, diseased, twisted, locked, or bent! This opened up tremendous possibilities.

We were glad to meet a full gospel Christian chiropractor who later confirmed that this was a genuine miracle known to him. Of course, the legs did not increase in length, but the hipbones became readjusted as soon as the spinal column was made straight.

WE HEAR EVERYWHERE THAT OTHERS ARE BELIEVING FOR THE SAME MIRACLES, AND GOD IS WORKING QUIETLY AND SMOOTHLY. THIS IS A BEGINNING OF "GREATER WORKS." HOW GREAT THEY WILL BECOME WHEN WE EXERCISE MORE DARING FAITH TO SEE GREATER MIRACLES.

We began to ask for those who had pains in their head, neck, back, thighs, legs, and feet to receive the laying on of hands in anticipation of this miracle. I can only say that the results in the last five years have been tremendous. We hear everywhere that others are believing for the same miracles, and God is working quietly and smoothly. This is a beginning of "greater works." How great they will become when we exercise more daring faith to see greater miracles. This miracle is but the beginning of greater miracles. It is hard for those who are bound in wheelchairs, for they have lost so much faith and hope, but their day is coming fast.

It was in Sydney, Australia, in November 1973, that an unusual miracle took place. A lady present had seen cases of leg lengthening and had been most impressed, for this was relatively new in Australia. Some had heard about it, but were very wary of it. This lady had a bent nose and had apparently never been able to breathe properly through either nostril. She asked me to pray for her bent nose. I laid my clumsy hands right on her nose and prayed in Jesus's name. The Lord immediately straightened the nose and she began breathing freely through both nostrils for the first time in her memory.

On the same tour, I was asked to pray for a young lady who had diseased and inflamed hips, which caused her to walk with difficulty. She called it *synovitis*. I asked my wife to lay hands on this girl's hips while I laid my hands on her head and prayed. Her hipbones began to move under my wife's hands. She said it felt uncanny! A naturopath doctor standing right behind testified that he could see the bones in the hips moving as we prayed.

Just a week before writing this chapter, in our Deeper Life Convention in Toronto, I prayed for a woman who was facing an operation for a degenerated hip. In this case, I sat her on the pew, for she was hobbling and hardly able to walk. I held her feet in my hands and one leg was "way off." I then prayed. Both legs began to move, mysteriously, and as the very hands of Jesus performed that awesome miracle, the hip joints came into place—she felt them moving. Her legs grew about one inch or more, and then she walked down the aisle and actually ran a few steps. These miracles are real.

In the next chapter, we will consider the miracle in the Bible that is our proof text—the healing of the lady with the double curvature of the spine. If it happened in Bible days, it should happen today if we will believe. All things are possible to them that believe.

3

MIRACLES AND DISEASE

Then a great multitude followed Him, because they saw His signs
which He performed on those who were diseased.
—John 6:2

In modern evangelism, the success of the campaign is usually determined by the crowds. In fact, every effort will be made to bring on special singers or special spectaculars to attract crowds. Of course, the whole crusade has to be paid for, so the greater the crowd the greater the offering. This syndrome is in accordance with the mind of man. It is, frankly, a psychological approach. John 3:16, with variations, will be faithfully preached, an appeal made, and decision cards filled out. Much good work has been done and genuine conversions have taken place—but did Jesus do it this way? Did He expect us to do it our way?

The reason that *"a great multitude followed Him"* was not caused by singers, spectacles, or gimmicks, but by miracles. Again, the word used is *semeion*, so the healing of diseases is described as supernatural signs, which were supposed to alert people and to attract their attention. Organized religion could not do these miracles, and had no desire to do them. They offered forms and ritual instead. Jesus invited sick people to come to Him, and He healed them all. Thus, the healing of sickness is clearly defined as God's miracle-working power, and was done to bring blessing to the people, and I can think of no greater method than this to get a crowd! Free healing for great multitudes!

"And Jesus went about all Galilee, teaching in their synagogues, preaching the gospel of the kingdom, and healing all kinds of sickness and all kinds of disease among the people" (Matthew 4:23). If the healing of a disease is a miracle, then we must discover what is meant by the word *disease*. It simply means to have been deprived of ease—in other words, to be unwell. From the Greek words used in the New Testament, we get the variant meanings: "want of strength, weakness, unsoundness, sickness, to feel bad, to be ill." The literal meaning of the word *sozo*, which is often translated *"saved"* in the Bible, is actually "to be made whole." Thus, the salvation brought by Jesus through His death on the cross was soundness and wholeness instead of disease, in both mind and body.

The manifestation of this salvation upon the Jews is called the working of miracles on those who were diseased.

Toward the end of 1974, I began to be made aware by the Spirit of God that we were approaching a time of a greater manifestation of God's miracle-working power throughout the church and the world. It must be appreciated that renewal of the church without miracles is a meaningless expression. Instead of a miracle only occurring very occasionally in history, more often by the sovereignty of God than the faith of man, we must expect that miracles will be the *normal* manifestation of God's glory in the church. Our big problem has been twofold. First, our clergy have not preached for miracles, neither have they expected them. Second, the evangelicals have taken a broad position called *dispensationalism*, which admits that Jesus worked miracles in His day but that they cannot and will not occur today. This is a theological cop-out. The liberals have not believed for miracles in any age. Neither did the Pharisees or the Sadducees. This is plain unbelief.

I began studying again the purpose of miracles in the church, and as I studied, I began preaching about them and expecting to see a greater manifestation of God's power. If I preached it, I had faith to expect it, and it began to open up. However, the second great obstacle was the tremendous unbelief of the people to whom I preached. They were not conditioned for miracles in their thinking. Most of them were in a denominational rut, and they did not expect to get out. The Son of God, with all His omnipotence, could do no miracles in His own hometown. *"He did not do many **mighty works** there because of their unbelief"* (Matthew 13:58). This means that He did a very few miracles only, because the word for *"mighty works"* is *dunamis*. In the very town of Nazareth, where Jesus was known by the residents as a "hometown boy," they were offended by Him. They said He was only a carpenter's son, and His mother was well known. Jesus first went into their synagogue and *taught them*; then He performed *"mighty works"* or miracles. Instead of praising God for using their hometown boy in such a way, they reasoned among themselves, "Where did He get this wisdom? From the Nazareth High School? How did He heal the sick?" There was no medical school in Nazareth. He showed amazing wisdom. Could He have gotten a master's degree in philosophy? But where? Certainly not in Nazareth. His glory was veiled because of their unbelief, because they were a small-town people with small-town minds. They were confined by parochialism and the teaching of their priests. I think there is a parallel in our denominational churches today—restrictive parochialism with a great bias of unbelief. Thank God, the Holy Spirit is breaking through the bonds of sectarianism and setting people free.

I started preaching and teaching for more miracles in my home church. I had the people come to the front and believe for their miracle. The first Sunday, it seemed that all who came, about ten, received very quick healings. Legs were lengthened, minor things like pains disappeared instantly. Yes, the removal of a headache in a split second is a miracle. It takes three aspirins much longer. One is a supernatural, mighty act of God; the other is healing by medical means.

I then traveled to Port Arthur, Texas, to a charismatic group in the city. I preached for miracles. To my astonishment, a lady came for prayer with cataracts on the eyes, and two minutes later, while still praying for people, my attention was drawn to this same lady who was calmly sitting in a pew reading her Bible—a thing she had been unable to do for years. Greatly encouraged, the next person I prayed for was partly deaf in both ears. Instantly, she heard perfectly. Next to her was another case of deafness in one ear, and this also yielded to the prayer of faith. Legs were lengthened and there was great joy in that church. One lady whose leg was lengthened was wearing a built-up shoe. After prayer, she no longer needed it. Remember that when Philip went to Samaria, the same thing happened and there was great joy in that city as well! We will soon find that miracles in the local church will spread to miracles in the marketplaces, or city squares, of the big cities. This is God's time to move. Are we ready to move with Him?

OUR BIG PROBLEM HAS BEEN TWOFOLD. FIRST, OUR CLERGY HAVE NOT PREACHED FOR MIRACLES, NEITHER HAVE THEY EXPECTED THEM. SECOND, THE EVANGELICALS HAVE TAKEN A BROAD POSITION CALLED *DISPENSATIONALISM*, WHICH ADMITS THAT JESUS WORKED MIRACLES IN HIS DAY BUT THAT THEY CANNOT AND WILL NOT OCCUR TODAY.

From Port Arthur, I traveled to Peterborough, Ontario, a city about ninety miles northeast of Toronto, where I was to speak to the local chapter of the Full Gospel Businessmen's Fellowship. Usually I give my personal testimony of God's progressive dealings in my life, but this time, I felt strongly urged to preach on miracles, and to encourage the people to believe for them. I told them of the visible miracle of spine straightening and leg adjusting that inspires such great faith. I explained that if they could *see* a miracle of this type, what were we to imagine happened inside the body among organs that we could not see? Then, realizing that there were over two hundred people present, I called for six volunteers who really believed. I got eighteen. The first lady had her leg lengthened one-half inch. She wept for joy—in fact, they all wept for joy! The next lady was paralyzed. She could not move her left arm and dragged her left foot. After praying for her, I told her to start moving her paralyzed arm, which she did, swinging it in increasing circles above her head; then she started to move her legs as in marching. Finally, she took off and walked easily round the assembled throng of praising people. This was very encouraging.

We soon came to one in the line who admitted to having a congenital diseased hip. Her left leg was *two inches* shorter, and she wore a two-inch lift in her shoe. I frankly wondered whether a degenerated hip would react quickly to the prayer of faith. I prayed and nothing moved. I then started to explain that miracles sometimes occurred more gradually over a period of weeks or months. They were miracles nevertheless. While I was explaining, the leg grew two inches before my eyes, and before a whole lot of other people who were eagerly watching. I held up the shoe for all to see the two-inch heel, and I told the woman that she must not wear these shoes again, and by God's provision, another woman present remembered that she had a spare pair of shoes in her car. She retrieved them and gave them to the newly healed woman—they fit her exactly.

The next in line was a woman claiming to have multiple sclerosis of the spine. She was sitting, so I had no time to get her to demonstrate her weakness or disease, but after prayer and the adjustment of her spinal column to its normal position, she wept for joy believing she was healed. All eighteen people received their miracle.

Two weeks later, I received a letter from a young woman stating that the people who watched were openly weeping. They had never seen anything like it, nor ever expected to. She called it "the day that miracles came to Peterborough." A Presbyterian minister from Port Hope, Ontario, was present and was going back to his church expecting miracles. Why not? I was raised a Presbyterian! God loves them. Later, this minister brought his wife to our church. She was wearing a built-up shoe and the Lord lengthened her leg also.

While on the subject of gradual miracles, I well remember the infant daughter of a gospel singer and his wife in Toronto. It happened several years ago, after we had attended a gospel service in the band shell at the Toronto exhibition grounds. This little girl was born with one leg withered. It was about two to three inches shorter than the other. I felt the compassion of the Lord and offered to pray for her in the open air. Her leg was whole within six months.

Of course, I realize that in writing a book like this, many may think that the working of miracles is something that ought to happen to anyone. According to the Bible it can happen to anyone who believes. (See Mark 16:17.) Notice that the qualification is simple belief. The opposite is unbelief. If you expect a miracle, you must state you expect it. This will be your confession of faith, Let us hear from Paul:

> *"The word is near you, **in your mouth** and in your heart" (that is, **the word of faith** which we preach): that if you **confess with your mouth** the Lord Jesus and believe in your heart that God has raised Him from the dead, you **will be saved**. For with the heart one believes unto righteousness, and **with the mouth** confession is made unto salvation.* (Romans 10:8–10)

This is a tremendously important passage of Scripture. First, the word of faith comes from our heart into our mouth. If it is not spoken it produces no results. It must be spoken. It must be confessed with the mouth, and this confession produces salvation; that is, it produces the miracle that makes a person whole, from his state of disease. The confession must be a bold confession, and the word spoken is *faith speaking*. Jesus explained it this way: *"Whosoever says to this mountain, 'Be removed and be cast into the sea,' and does not doubt in his heart, but believes that those things he says will be done,* **he will have whatever he says**" (Mark 11:23).

The receiving of your miracle not only rests upon what Jesus did in shedding His blood on Calvary, but it also rests on your personal verbal confession of what you expect will happen to you, based on the law of love of Calvary. Instead of confessing pain, disease, weakness, misery, hoping you will be healed, you must boldly come to Jesus confessing your miracle. (See Hebrews 10:19.) Our problem today is this lack of boldness, and the inarticulate confession of most church-going people. If you want a mountain miracle, you must make a bold confession. "Please pray for me. I believe the mountain in my life will go away—I really do, so help me, God."

4

THE MIRACLE OF THE LOGOS

And everyone present was filled with the Holy Spirit and
began speaking in languages they didn't know,
for the Holy Spirit gave them this ability.
—Acts 2:4 TLB

In order to understand the miracle of the *Logos*—the spoken Word—we must consider the Virgin Mary and her two experiences of the Holy Spirit. As recorded in Luke, chapter 1, the angel Gabriel informed Mary that the Holy Spirit would overshadow her and the result of this intimate embrace would be the conception of the Son of God. This enveloping in a shroud of glory would cause a supernatural miracle to take place—the creation and placing of the very Christ in the virgin's womb. In the due course of gestation, the beautiful body of the Christ was born into this world—Jesus, the Son of God. This Man had to wait thirty years before He was anointed of the Holy Spirit as prophesied by Daniel. (See Daniel 9:24.) Then, and only then, did this miracle Man begin a demonstration of miracles. For three-and-a-half years, this miracle Man lived a miracle life and produced miracles at every turn. This is still the purpose of the anointed body of Christ today. This is why God is pouring out His Spirit upon all flesh today.

The word *logos* is used in John 1:1 and 14. *"In the beginning was the Word, and the Word was with God, and the Word was God…. And the Word became flesh and dwelt among us."* This describes Jesus, the Son of God, as the *Logos*, or the living, vital Word of God. This same Word that proceeded from the Father in Genesis 1 and 2, and brought forth creation, was placed into a human body, and after Jesus was anointed of the Father by the Holy Spirit in the Jordan River (see Matthew 3:16), this Word was manifest supernaturally. First, the Father *spoke* saying, *"This is My beloved Son, in whom I am well pleased"* (Matthew 3:17). Then, the Son continued to manifest the Word, which He received from His Father, for Jesus became the Living Word veiled in His human body. Every time He opened His mouth, out came the living Word of God. It is this living Word that creates miracles. He spoke and it was done. The people's officers said, *"No man ever spoke like this Man!"* (John 7:46). These Jewish elders had never heard the Word of God proceeding out of a human. They had only heard the dead theological letter of the law. This Word spoken brought fife where death reigned. It was, and is, a creative Word. The people said that He taught as one who had authority, not like the religious priests. (See Mark 1:22.)

This Word of life, spoken by Jesus in the synagogue in Capernaum, challenged the demons in a man, and they started to cry out. Demons will always oppose the living Word.

The work of Mary in giving birth to the Son of God was not finished at Bethlehem, for, thirty-three-and-a-half years later, she went into the upper room in Jerusalem, for Jesus had commanded her to wait for the promise of the Father, which was the baptism with the Holy Spirit. (See Acts 1:4–5.) She had no idea what would happen when she and 119 others received this "baptism with the Holy Spirit." It was a mystery to her, as it is to thousands today, but she did not back off, but obediently went into the upper room, which was to become the maternity ward of the church.

After ten days of prayer, the Day of Pentecost arrived, and suddenly the Holy Spirit descended a *second time* on the head of the Virgin Mary. As soon as this heavenly embrace was felt, she brought forth the living Word of God—the *Logos*. The first time, she gave birth to God's Son. Now, she brought forth the Word of her Son. Her Son spoke! It was the same creative, healing, miracle-working Word that He had spoken while on earth. Now, His church—His body—was to continue the same ministry. By the baptism with the Holy Spirit, Mary could now do the miracles that her Son had wrought in His flesh.

Every child born into this world must cry out to express its God-given life. The maternity wards of hospitals are full of crying infants. The infant church also cried out, expressing its newfound spiritual life. The cry that was heard was the voice of Jesus speaking supernaturally through His mother and 119 other disciples. As He waited for the anointing of the same Spirit to begin His ministry on earth, so likewise His disciples had to wait in the upper room for their anointing to do the works of Jesus. That we might be in no doubt as to what this experience meant to them, we must remember that Jesus had told them that His followers would not only do the works that He did, but that they would do greater works and miracles. (See John 14:12.) This is the day for the greater miracles to be done by the church as it is progressively restored to its former power and format. Miracles are soon to be the order of our day.

THIS IS THE DAY FOR THE GREATER MIRACLES TO BE DONE BY THE CHURCH AS IT IS PROGRESSIVELY RESTORED TO ITS FORMER POWER AND FORMAT. MIRACLES ARE SOON TO BE THE ORDER OF OUR DAY.

We have already referred to the operation of the Word of faith spoken from the mouth of believers. (See Romans 10:8–10.) This is a true expression of the *Logos* spoken from the heart through the mouth. It creates its own confession. As God spoke in Genesis 1, and creation took place, so also, as we speak the Word of faith, we may expect to see creative miracles, if we do not doubt in our heart. This is the obstacle that prevents miracles—unbelief in our heart. Remember that faith is a gift of God, one of the nine charismatic gifts enumerated in 1 Corinthians 12:8–10. If faith is a supernaturally implanted gift, then it creates of its kind, that is, it creates supernaturally. The Roman centurion knew this rule, for he said to Jesus, *"But only speak a word, and my servant will be healed"* (Matthew 8:8). Jesus opened His mouth and said, *"'Go your way; and as you have believed, so let it be done for you.' And his servant was healed that same hour."* (verse 13). What healed the servant? The Word of God (*Logos*) that created life, because the centurion released this Logos by his faith. His gift of faith as spoken pressed the trigger that sent the life-giving Word from heaven. It was just as easy for God to heal the servant as to swing the sun into place. All He does is speak. All we have to do is speak—in faith. It is no use at all speaking empty words. They must be supernatural words released by our gift of faith; then the word becomes the Word of faith.

It must be admitted that speaking in languages that we have not learned is a miracle. It is called a sign (*semeion*) miracle in Mark 16:17. The experience is for all believers. In fact, as I understand the Bible, all believers *must* have this evidence of the baptism with the Holy Spirit to do the works of Jesus and work miracles. This list of miracles in Mark 16 includes the casting out of demons, speaking in unknown languages, handling deadly demonic situations, absorbing evil poisonous things by natural and spiritual ingestion, and healing the sick and diseased. Every single one of the (*semeion*) signs is a supernatural miracle, and they all follow the believer; and this supernatural miracle-working ministry begins with the living Word (*Logos*) coming forth from our mouths, supernaturally speaking divine words of praise to God that we never learned naturally. Speaking in tongues is a supreme miracle, and one that begins a whole chain reaction of miracles, such as interpretation of tongues, prophecy, the word of knowledge and of wisdom, discernment of spirits and, of course, healing and the working of miracles. The life of a true Spirit-filled believer is one continuing miracle.

As in the case of Mary, who brought forth the Son of God, so likewise, when the Spirit of God moves upon us initially and woos us and we accept Jesus as our Savior, the Holy Spirit implants Jesus in our hearts or innermost parts. Jesus becomes the new Tenant and Controller of our lives. But in order that His power might be released, we must be saturated with the Holy Spirit, and this second work of the Holy Spirit in our lives produces the outflow of the Word—the *Logos*. This is why Jesus prophesied that rivers of living water would come out of our innermost parts. It is interesting that the Son of God is called *"the Word"* in heaven in 1 John 5:7, but called *"water"* in verse 8. The Word in heaven becomes the flowing river of life through us on earth. The Word in us must always be manifest as a flowing, life-giving verbal expression. Like Jesus, we speak and it is done. Water in a jug remaining static will get foul, but flowing water from the river of God (see Revelation 22:1) is always fresh and pure and will give life wherever it flows. This fountain of living water is desperately needed today to flow into the barren churches. This is why, in Psalm 68:9, the psalmist writes, *"You, O God, sent a plentiful rain, whereby You confirmed Your inheritance, when it was weary."* This is God's true confirmation service, when Jesus the great Bishop lays His hands on us and we manifest His life in speaking in other languages. This brings great refreshment when we are weary, so Paul admonishes us to edify or refresh ourselves by speaking in tongues. (See 1 Corinthians 14:4.)

If all believers would open their mouths each morning on awakening and praise God in their unknown tongue, we would almost have the dawn of the millennium upon us. It may well be that this will be the spiritual state of the church in our generation, when Jesus has built it back without spot or wrinkle or any such thing. (See Ephesians 5:27.) I am convinced that those who daily greet the Lord in tongues have less problems with depression, worrying, and consequent physical sicknesses. Many who have had the baptism in the Spirit and have spoken freely in tongues later have been robbed by whisperings of Satan, either saying they can no longer praise in tongues or that it is a poor quality tongue, and thus, it dries up with discouragement. Oh, the subtleties of Satan and our gullibility in listening to him!

THE WORD IN HEAVEN BECOMES THE FLOWING RIVER OF LIFE THROUGH US ON EARTH. THE WORD IN US MUST ALWAYS BE MANIFEST AS A FLOWING, LIFE-GIVING VERBAL EXPRESSION. LIKE JESUS, WE SPEAK AND IT IS DONE.

I would rather be among those who overdo praise (if that is possible) than those who praise seldom but grumble much.

Isaiah knew it would happen. *"For I will pour water on him who is thirsty, and floods on the dry ground; I will pour My Spirit on your descendants, My blessing on your offspring"* (Isaiah 44:3). Joel knew it too, for he prophesied of Christ, *"I will pour out My Spirit on all flesh; your sons and your daughters shall prophesy"* (Joel 2:28, see also Acts 2:17). As Jesus pours out His living Word upon His church today, it becomes alive, and each mouth of each believer becomes an orifice out of which this living Word flows to the thirsty multitudes who have been weary too long.

It is our mouths that He uses. Our bodies are the temple of the Holy Spirit, and it is from under the altar in heaven that this water flows and from under the altar of our heart (innermost parts) to the thirsty ones. We become water fountains in the wilderness, *"For waters shall burst forth in the wilderness, and streams in the desert"* (Isaiah 35:6). What a favored generation we are when God makes His church into one huge, life-giving fountain all over this barren world. Are you ready to overflow?

5

CONTROLLING THE ELEMENTS

Then He arose and rebuked the wind, and said to the sea, "Peace,
be still!" And the wind ceased and there was a great calm.
—Mark 4:39

This is a true story! It not only happened in those far-off days, but it
also happens today! Jesus has never changed. It is the church that has
changed in departing from its original power and authority. Jesus gave
the twelve apostles of the Lamb miracle power (*dunamis*) and authority
(*exousia*) over *all demons* and to cure diseases. (See Luke 9:1.) The same
legal authority and power was given to the seventy. (See Luke 10:1.) It
was later given to the whole church. (See Mark 16:16–20.) They did not
endure long years at a seminary learning negatives. They were given an
assignment that relied entirely upon their positive faith in Jesus. It was
very simple—to oppose all demonic forces wherever found and to cure
diseases. How simple! Notice that the Greek word for *"power"* is that
miracle word *dunamis*. It means that Jesus handed first to the twelve
apostles, then to the seventy evangelists, and lastly to the whole church
the ability to work acts of power, or miracles, wherever they ministered

His Word. Miracles and healings were to be the normal expectation of their ministry. First preach, then heal, then cast out demons and raise the dead. (See Matthew 10:7–8.) If you put your faith and confidence in John 3:16, or any other Scripture, by logic, you must have faith in any other promise or command in the Bible, especially if Jesus spoke it.

> *And they went out and preached everywhere, the Lord working with them and confirming the word* [Logos] *through the accompanying signs.* (Mark 16:20)

Let me pause for a moment and tell you of two miracles that happened between the fourth and fifth chapters of this book. This chapter is being written on a Monday at the beginning of December 1974. Yesterday was Sunday, and as usual, people we had not seen before came to the church for a miracle. They could not receive it in their home churches, but they exercised faith and came. A German-speaking man came forward for prayer. He had injured his back in a German coalmine twenty years ago. The pain was so bad that he frequently had to roll out of bed in the mornings; to take a bath he had somehow to roll into the bathtub. He had pain in the back in the region of the kidneys. Let us see what Jesus did to this man in five minutes. I sat him down on the front pew of the church in full view of the congregation. His left leg was half an inch shorter than the right, a frequent trouble in back injuries. While we held his feet and prayed, Jesus caused the shorter leg to grow longer than the left leg; then the left leg began to grow and both ended up equal. This meant that a miracle of spine straightening had taken place. He explained that his kidney area hurt badly, so my hand was laid on him, the pain rebuked in Jesus's name and commanded to go away. While still holding my hand on his back, I asked the congregation if they believed this pain would go—they all agreed fervently, the man agreed, and I agreed. I took my hand away and commanded him to touch his toes. He hesitated but I encouraged him, and he did so, touching the ground. He arose with a look of curious wonder on his face, for all pain had gone and the act of touching his toes was a thing he had been absolutely unable to do in twenty years. Seeing that Satan was on the run, I asked, "Have you received the baptism in the Holy Spirit?" He said he had not, so I again laid my hands on him and almost immediately the Holy Spirit came upon him and he began to praise God in a new language, which he called "a prayer language." He then turned to the congregation and told them in English and German (for some of our people speak German) that God had given him three miracles—all in five minutes.

After that, I faced a lady from a city in Ontario called Peterborough, where miracles had been performed a few weeks earlier. This lady had continual head pains, neck pains, and weakness. First, she sat down, and again her left leg was half an inch shorter than the right, and so I held her feet and prayed, but there was only a very small movement. I had seen this before, so I asked her to stand and then placed my hands on her head and prayed against the head oppression, then on the back of the neck and commanded these pains to go in Jesus's name. At this point she sank to the floor under the incoming miracle-working power of God and lay there peacefully for a minute while Jesus did the necessary internal physical operation by His Spirit. I then asked her if she would like to receive the baptism in the Holy Spirit, and quietly she replied in the affirmative. Again, I laid hands on her head and she immediately began to speak in tongues as the Spirit gave her the utterance. Then I again examined her leg length, and now they were both absolutely equal. It had a tremendous effect on her son who accompanied her. This is why Jesus does miracles today. I asked the lady about her church affiliation, and, a little to my surprise, she said, "I am just about to join the Roman Catholic Church." I said, "Praise the Lord, and God bless you." She was weeping. God is moving everywhere today!

Some years ago, around 1958, Toronto was visited with a tremendous snowstorm. In a few hours, three feet of snow lay everywhere and some of the drifts were six to eight feet high. This naturally caused all traffic to come to a halt! It cost the city of Toronto one million dollars to clear up the mess. Three days later, a report came over the radio that a storm of similar intensity was approaching from Pennsylvania and it was expected to dump an equal load of snow on our city. This was the day of our weekly prayer meeting, so as we were worshipping, the Lord put into my heart a gift of faith. I suggested to the small congregation that we agree together in prayer to stop the expected snowstorm. We rose to our feet, and I raised my hands toward heaven and said, "I rebuke the storm in the name of Jesus and command it not to visit our city!" At the time of its expected arrival, there was a small dusting of snow, and then it stopped. An announcement came over the radio that for reasons that could not be explained, the expected storm had split into two while crossing Lake Ontario, completely missing Toronto and dumping its load on the farm lands in Ontario, where it was badly needed. One of the women there telephoned the weather bureau at the airport and asked them if they would like to know why this happened. They said they were interested, and she proceeded to tell them the whole story! The man thanked her and suggested we might be useful on future occasions in controlling the weather! Jesus stopped a storm by rebuking the wind and the waves!

THE TROUBLE WITH MOST CHRISTIANS IS THAT THEY KNOW NOTHING OF THE REALITY OF AN INVISIBLE WORLD OF MALIGN SPIRITS, OPERATING UNDER THE DIRECT COMMAND OF SATAN, THEIR PRINCE.

How is it that wind, waves, and snow obey a command given in Jesus's name? Is the miracle explainable? Not by natural science, of course, but when we understand the principles involved it becomes clear. I have already quoted the words of Jesus giving His commission to His disciples, that they could have His miracle power over all demons. The trouble with most Christians is that they know nothing of the reality of an invisible world of antagonistic spirits operating under the direct command of Satan, their prince. Satan is described as: (1) the prince of the world (see John 12:31), and (2) the prince of the power of *the air* (see Ephesians 2:2). God is the author of peace and order, not confusion. A storm represents destruction and confusion, and Satan is behind a storm. This may not sound scientific, but when a believer operating the gift of faith rebukes a storm, in effect he rebukes and binds the demonic forces actually causing the wind to blow, the waters to surge and the snow to descend in volume. A Christian who does not understand this principle would not even attempt to work such a miracle!

In Mel Tari's book, *The Gentle Breeze of Jesus*, he tells of a team of Christian workers who hired a boat owned by Muslims to visit an offshore island off Timor, Indonesia. Between this island and the mainland was a dangerous whirlpool that had sucked many to their death. The journey was quite safe in calm weather, for they skirted the danger, but on this occasion, a terrible storm arose and they were being inexorably drawn into the whirlpool. One of the young Christian men heard the voice of the Lord telling him that He would deliver them all safely if he would take dominion over the storm in Jesus's name. The young man was obedient to the Lord and informed the Muslim skipper that the Lord had told him to tell the skipper that he was to stop bailing and trying to save both boat and crew and give the matter to this young Christian. Of course, the captain was completely contemptuous of this young man and showed it with hostility; but after a few more minutes of hopeless struggling against the forces of nature on the rampage, he gave up, knowing that they would all drown in the whirlpool. It was then, and only then, that the young man said, "I told you to stop struggling and let me do it, as the Lord showed me." So then he stood to his feet, openly rebuked the storm in Jesus's name, and commanded it to stop. *Instantly* the sea became deadly calm, and the only evidence that there had been a storm was the foam floating on top of the calm water. The wind stopped instantly and the sea was like a millpond, because a young man believed God. This miracle so shocked the Muslim crew that they all accepted Jesus Christ as their Savior that day, acknowledging that no other God could work such a miracle. It takes miracles today to change the world. Miracles will be seen on television and will be done before millions, and millions will believe on the Son of God. This is what church renewal is all about.

In 1970, my wife and I were invited to teach in the Bible School of Christ for the Nations Institute in Dallas, Texas. We had our airline tickets, but on the morning of departure a fog developed. It was a bad one. We phoned Toronto airport, but they assured us that all was "go." On arriving at the airport a half-hour later, however, the fog had worsened and we were informed at the desk of American Airlines that their plane coming in from Chicago had been diverted to Buffalo. This left a United Airlines plane still in the air en route for Toronto. They told us that if this plane could land, we would be transferred to it. I sat waiting and took my wife's hand in agreement and we commanded that United Airlines plane to land *and* take off. The next we heard was that this plane was circling the airport trying to seek a way in, but then the announcer on the PA system said that all planes were unable to land and recommended that people return to their homes or seek hotel accommodation. I looked at my wife and she said that it looked as if this miracle had failed for the first time. I refused to accept this, and again took her hand and prayed, "Lord, I have commanded this plane to land in Your name and take off again with us, and I believe it will be so according to our prayer." A few minutes later, this plane loomed up through the fog outside the window. In ten minutes we were aboard and it roared away through the fog en route to Chicago, as far as I know, the *only plane* to land and take off after the announcement in the airport building. You see, I have never missed an appointment for the Lord. He controls the elements, but we have to do the commanding!

Another incident comes to mind. I was due to speak in a conference in Champaign, Illinois, but we had had a strike of technicians at the Toronto airport and the timetables of scheduled flights had been thrown haywire. After a half-hour delay, I entered the aircraft and, as soon as we were comfortably settled in, an announcement came over the intercom stating that this plane would not take off for one-and-a-half hours. I would therefore miss the connections at Chicago and not arrive in time for the first ministry of the Word. I closed my eyes and said quietly, "Lord, in Your name, I command this plane to take off." Instantly, the same captain of the aircraft switched on the intercom again and said, "Ladies and gentlemen, we are about to take off right now." It quickly taxied to the runway and was away. I caught my connecting flight out of Chicago and arrived on time. When Satan sees we are working for the Lord, he tries to stop us, but as we oppose him in the Master's name, he has to give way and let go and retreat. This is what James had in mind when he wrote, *"Resist the devil and he will flee from you"* (James 4:7). Have you ever tried? It always works.

What wonderful days we are living in today—the times of the restoration of the true church to all its original power and beauty.

IT TAKES MIRACLES TODAY TO CHANGE THE WORLD. MIRACLES WILL BE SEEN ON TELEVISION AND WILL BE DONE BEFORE MILLIONS, AND MILLIONS WILL BELIEVE ON THE SON OF GOD. THIS IS WHAT CHURCH RENEWAL IS ALL ABOUT.

6

A CHRISTIAN'S SAFETY

Behold, I give unto you power [exousia, authority]...over all the
power of the enemy: and nothing shall by any means hurt you.
—Luke 10:19 KJV

In 1948, when the Lord began to open up my eyes to see the amazing authority that He has vested in us to work miracles, the above Scripture became extremely important. I was being used as a pioneer in what is now called "the deliverance ministry." I began casting out evil spirits from people who were cruelly bound by the enemy, and I saw with my own eyes, tremendous miracles of healing of the body and mind taking place. The first three miracles, in order, were deliverance from asthma, suicide, and epilepsy. These three people are still healed today, over thirty years later. It works.

Having proved that we had the authority of Jesus to do these things, we suddenly realized that we were far out on a theological limb. No one understood. Other pastors in the city began to shun us and I was no longer acceptable on the Toronto Full Gospel ministerial. To be alone (with my wife, of course) and to be far out on this limb in 1948 seemed to be a dangerous position. This became especially obvious when Satan attacked my wife and me in the middle of the night by trying to stop our hearts from beating. We were cautioned to stop this ministry. I remember telling the Lord in prayer that if this amazing, miraculous ministry meant that I would lose my life, I was willing to die for His sake. From that time onward, and by facing Satan squarely in Jesus's name and honoring His precious blood, I won through to a deliverance ministry that, I am told, has influenced many men of God to do the same. What did Jesus say? *"Nothing shall by any means hurt you"*! Nothing, absolutely nothing. No disease, no problem, no storm, no marriage problem, no financial disaster—nothing. Does this really apply to us? Yes, all of us. This means to hurt, to harm, or to injure, and includes the whole area of accidents!

From 1948 to this year of 1979, I have found Jesus to be true to this promise. We speak the word of faith coming from our hearts through the mouth directed against Satan, and he retreats! He runs away before the blast from heaven that honors the name of Jesus, the blood of Jesus and the Word of God, for we read a most simple statement of the early Christian martyrs—*"they overcame him* [Satan] *by the blood of the Lamb, and by the word of their testimony"* (Revelation 12:11). It was the living blood of Jesus (for His life is in His blood) and the Logos Word, Jesus Himself, spoken out of their mouths that drove back Satan and his demonic cohorts. Victory after victory occurred. Jesus is Victor, and so are we *in Him*. Your present life of defeat can change into a life of continual victory.

Those who overcame Satan in the early church were not always delivered from death or torture. They were promoted to a higher order of life through death, for it is written of them, *"And they overcame him* [Satan] *by the blood of the Lamb, and by the word of their testimony; and they did not love their lives to the death"* (Revelation 12:11). Losing their life was the means of gaining their life in the next. If they had denied their Savior while facing persecution, they would have forfeited eternal life, for Jesus said that if we deny Him in this life, our Father, who is in heaven, will deny us. (See Matthew 10:33.) In our generation, it is more likely that we shall be delivered out of our troubles in this life if we are faced with persecution for our testimony. Either way, in life or death, we glorify God and maintain our victory in Christ. There is no sting in death or life in Christ.

If Jesus said that nothing would hurt us or harm us or bring us injury, He meant it. It is true, for He is truth.

IN OUR GENERATION, IT IS MORE LIKELY THAT WE SHALL BE DELIVERED OUT OF OUR TROUBLES IN THIS LIFE IF WE ARE FACED WITH PERSECUTION FOR OUR TESTIMONY. EITHER WAY, IN LIFE OR DEATH, WE GLORIFY GOD AND MAINTAIN OUR VICTORY IN CHRIST. THERE IS NO STING IN DEATH OR LIFE IN CHRIST.

A woman who had worshipped in our church before working as a nurse in Chicago, was suddenly accosted one evening by two youths, one of whom was wielding a knife. She saw the youth approaching with the open knife pointing at her stomach. Her first reaction was to freeze, but then she remembered her authority as a child of God and she spoke the Word. She said, "I plead the blood of Jesus against you, and I rebuke you in Jesus's name." Then, lunging forward, she said, "Give me that knife," and the youth released it into her hand. She then moved toward him, and said, "You stand right there." Then she commanded the second young man, *in the name of Jesus*, to go into an adjacent building and telephone the police to come and pick the boys up. He immediately obeyed her command. When the police came, the second boy ran away. The police picked up the boy who was being held up at knifepoint and later picked up the other boy also. The woman was unharmed because Jesus said, "*Nothing shall by any means hurt you.*"

Every air hijack attempt could be thwarted if there was just one Son of God on board who knew his authority over the demonic forces that work against humanity. If Satan can't stop an aircraft taking off, he can't bring one down either, if he is commanded not to do so. Just imagine what will happen in this world when the church—the body of Christ—is fully restored.

Faith is the opposite of fear. Where faith reigns, fear cannot operate, but where fear is present, with all its disastrous torments, ulcers, and nervous tensions, the devil reaps a full harvest at your expense. It is about time we learned to turn the tables on Satan, to command him *not* to do the things he does and to take his dirty hands off our minds and bodies. Peter meant exactly what he said. "*Be sober, be vigilant; because your adversary the devil walks about like a roaring lion, seeking whom he may devour. Resist him, steadfast in the faith*" (1 Peter 5:8–9). How many Christians can you find doing this? How many are giving place to Satan, giving way, giving up, giving in? He knows our weaknesses and takes every advantage against us, but Jesus has made a provision for us all. He said, "*Nothing shall by any means hurt you.*" Why, then, do we get hurt? Our aches, pains, problems, and troubles seem to deny the words of Jesus. We read them but they do not work. We get discouraged, maybe because our pastor doesn't teach the Word, even though he claims to believe the entire Bible. We have doctors and psychiatrists, so why bother Jesus?

It was on the cross that Jesus purchased our entire salvation, which means "soundness," from the Greek *soteria*. He purchased total soundness for spirit, soul, and body of mankind—all mankind, but only those who dare to believe may enter into the benefits of this so great salvation, otherwise "*how shall we escape?*" (Hebrews 2:3).

We can't go around demonstrating miracles "just for fun." This is a serious business. It is only when we are faced with danger and the enemy is at the gates of our lives that we use the authority Jesus has given to us. It is for emergency use only, like the emergency door in an aircraft. When danger strikes, we have the victory and immediate recourse to all the help of the Father, Son, and Holy Spirit, plus uncounted angels who will leap to the defense of the man or woman who says, "I come against you, adversary, in Jesus's name." Let us remember, however, that Jesus will not act until we take the initiative in His name to precipitate the miracle. This is why He commanded His disciples to preach and then *heal...exorcise.* This is why we are told to lay our hands on the sick so that they shall recover, because our hands become the extension of His hands from heaven, we being members of the body of Christ, acting with His authority and power. Through our mouth comes the word of faith, sounding like Gabriel's horn, and through our hands is transmitted the necessary power (*dunamis,* miracle power) to work the miracle.

Any pastor, worker, or believer can do these things. This book is being written to help to encourage and stir up the faith of those who read, to join together and force Satan out of many of his strongholds. Begin in yourself. Command Satan to get out of your mind, your body, your life. Then turn your power and authority on Satan in your family. Drive him out of your home. Give no place to him anywhere; give him no quarter, no compromise; tell him you mean business at last; you have put up with him long enough. This is the day the Lord has made and you are going to rejoice in it instead of being sad and sorrowful in it.

I was talking to a Spirit-filled mailman recently. I asked him how he got on with his workmates. He said that at first they used to use the language normal to an unbelieving working man, but as he showed his love toward them and had opportunities of witness, they stopped swearing in his presence and the whole atmosphere of that post office changed. One man against the devil. He showed them love, he prayed for them quietly, he testified of God's goodness and they thawed. This is what is needed in every home and office—one who prays, binds the power of the devil, pleads the blood of Jesus; this will make it more uncomfortable for Satan to stick around. He will progressively leave.

Have you pastors tried this in cases of church problems and splits? The Holy Spirit brings unity always, but Satan divides. By this you will know what spirit is working in the midst of your congregation. The moment that Jesus went into the synagogue at Capernaum, demons started to cry out and oppose Him. He did not run away; He stayed to give the whole congregation a first-class demonstration of His power and authority. *"Jesus rebuked him, saying, 'Be quiet, and come out of him!'"* (Mark 1:25). There was no question as to who was the Master, for it is recorded that *"when the unclean spirit had convulsed him and cried out with a loud voice, he came out of him"* (verse 26). What a shock this would be if it happened in some of our churches today! I can see a lot of people scurrying out of the church as fast as their legs could carry them! Then again they said, "What new doctrine is this?" You see, their pastors had not taught them to expect this! The poor suffering man who needed Jesus's love and compassion would have remained bound by demons until his dying day unless Jesus had intervened. Do you realize what this means today in the restoration of the church? It means He has chosen us to be the deliverers to the church in His name. This is not the day for buck-passing or cop-outs. This is the day for positive action.

THIS IS WHAT IS NEEDED IN EVERY HOME AND OFFICE—ONE WHO PRAYS, BINDS THE POWER OF THE DEVIL, PLEADS THE BLOOD OF JESUS; THIS WILL MAKE IT MORE UNCOMFORTABLE FOR SATAN TO STICK AROUND. HE WILL PROGRESSIVELY LEAVE.

Moses long ago had to learn this lesson. No backing away, but taking hold of the serpent by the tail, twisting it and destroying it. (See Exodus 4.) The serpent is a type of Satan, and Jesus took him by the tail and twisted it at Calvary, and now He tells us to go and cast Satan out of every situation.

"*Behold I give you power* [authority] *to tread on...all the power of the enemy*" (Luke 10:19 KJV). How delightful to squelch the very life out of every demonic situation that we encounter, to put our feet (shod with the preparation of the gospel) on demons and sicknesses, and command the devil to surrender. David went one further long ago—he cut off Goliath's head and then stood on him. He knew in his day that it was true, as John said later, "*He who is in you is greater than he* [Satan] *who is in the world*" (1 John 4:4). Even though Satan is the prince of this world, Jesus has overcome the world for us.

We have only begun to touch the beginning of this great ministry of the working of miracles. It is one of the nine charismatic gifts of the Spirit mentioned in 1 Corinthians 12. With this charismatic renewal, we must have a full operation of all the nine charismatic manifestations of Christ. Miracles is an exciting one, and it is here.

A priest in one of my recent meetings in Florida saw demons coming out when I prayed, so, the next day, he met a woman who was sick. Remembering what I had said, and having seen how I had done it, he asked her permission to try. She agreed, so he put his hands on her head and roundly rebuked the sickness. The spirits of infirmity causing the bodily weakness came out with deep coughs. Afterward, she said, "Oh, I feel so much better now!" Yes, but what had he done? He had worked a miracle in bringing health to this lady by dislodging the cause of her sickness in Jesus's name.

In the same meeting, I was praying for a man and rebuking the unclean spirit behind the smoking habit that bound him. It began to come out with deep coughs, and a man, an unbeliever, sitting behind him, suddenly began to feel terrible. His pulse rate began to increase and he started to perspire and said it felt as if his head was about to burst. Why? Because the same unclean spirit was in him also. The pastor of the assembly explained this to him and asked if he were a Christian. On finding that he was not, the pastor pointed him to Christ, whom he readily accepted. Then the pastor cast out the unclean spirits, which came out quite readily, with coughing. Then, when he had been cleaned up and the vessel of his body was made ready, the pastor prayed for him and he began to speak in tongues as the Spirit came in. One miracle of deliverance precipitates another, until the domino theory goes into effect. Satan drops out of a number of situations. A miracle will always precipitate further blessings.

7

WALKING MIRACLES

Here am I and the children whom the LORD has given me! We are
for signs and wonders in Israel from the LORD of hosts.
—Isaiah 8:18

No doubt the primary reference to this Scripture is to Isaiah's own family, for he married a prophetess (see Isaiah 8:3), but Isaiah typified the Lord Jesus Christ, as do all the Old Testament prophets, and in the larger fulfillment of this prophecy, it refers to the Son of God as Head of His church, composed of many sons and daughters, whom the Father would give Him in the New Testament age. We see the same principle operating in the understanding of Bible prophecy, in which Isaiah speaks of God speaking to Israel by an alien people. If Israel refused to obey God, He would send foreign armies against them, and they would be unable to understand their language. This is the primary fulfillment, but in the New Testament Paul brought out this verse which reads, *"For with stammering lips and another tongue He will speak to this people...yet they would not hear"* (Isaiah 28:11–12), and interprets its fulfillment as the ability to speak in tongues, which all Spirit-filled Christians may enjoy. (See 1 Corinthians 14:21.)

As we project Isaiah 8:18 into the New Testament, it applies to Christians who are *in* Christ. Obviously, if New Testament Christians have measured up to the minimum requirements of Acts 2:38, which is the basis for their experience, then the threefold promise will be: (1) repentance, (2) water baptism, and (3) receiving the Holy Spirit—in that order. If this verse is taken by some to prove that all born-again believers received the Holy Spirit at conversion, I would ask the question as to whether they were also baptized in water at the instant of conversion. The order is obvious. The sinner receives Jesus as Savior and then identifies himself with Jesus in His death and resurrection by being immersed in water, and then the new believer may receive the baptism in the Spirit. In a previous chapter, I mentioned this happening to a person who reacted in the Baptist church in Florida where I was ministering when an unclean spirit was rebuked in another person. This man went through the first stage of repentance, then deliverance, and within ten minutes, spoke in tongues as the evidence that the Holy Spirit had come. Water baptism would follow in this case.

Anyone who speaks in tongues is a walking miracle. No wonder Satan hates this sign, for it is the outflowing of the River of Life from heaven. He will try to shut it off, dam it, and block the faucet if he possibly can. He hates tongues, for they manifest Jesus in spoken form. Our trouble in past centuries has been that many people who went to church were dead spiritually, or to be charitable, some had a spark of eternal life in them. Paul, writing about these very people, said, *"Having a form of godliness but denying its power [dunamis—miracle power]. And from such people turn away!"* (2 Timothy 3:5). These people go to a church that has a form of godliness. It has forms, liturgy, ceremonies and communion, but the leaders of these churches deny tongues, healing, and miracles. We are commanded to keep away from them, for their errors will quench our zeal. We must remember, and remember again and again, that the church *began* with tongues. It will end with tongues at the coming of Jesus. Those who oppose the miracle-working power (*dunamis*), which is supposed to be in the body of Christ, are, in reality, opposing Jesus. To have forms and traditions in churches but to deny His glorious power to baptize in the Spirit, to heal sicknesses of members of His body, to cast out demons from these people, is like going to a food store and coming home with empty bags full of air. We would soon die of starvation. We need fullness, the fullness of the Spirit, to satisfy our deepest longings.

TO HAVE FORMS AND TRADITIONS IN CHURCHES BUT TO DENY HIS GLORIOUS POWER TO BAPTIZE IN THE SPIRIT, TO HEAL SICKNESSES OF MEMBERS OF HIS BODY, TO CAST OUT DEMONS FROM THESE PEOPLE, IS LIKE GOING TO A FOOD STORE AND COMING HOME WITH EMPTY BAGS FULL OF AIR. WE WOULD SOON DIE OF STARVATION. WE NEED FULLNESS, THE FULLNESS OF THE SPIRIT, TO SATISFY OUR DEEPEST LONGINGS.

As we turn to our Scripture in Isaiah, we find that this was the same thought. Children of God were supposed to be miracle children. The very word used for "wonder" can be translated from the Hebrew as "miracle." All Christians are supposed to be walking miracles. One of the names of Jesus recorded by Isaiah 9:6 is Wonderful. It is because He was a miracle-working Man while on earth, and now He wants us to be miracle-working men and women while on earth. When Simeon prophesied over Mary, the mother of Jesus, he said that her Son would be for a *sign* (*semeion*—miracle) that would be spoken against. His whole life was a living miracle, and the leaders of the state religion hated Him because He did (and was) what they could not do and be. The contrast was too great. It was white light showing up black darkness.

> *And this is the condemnation, that the light has come into the world, and men loved darkness rather than light, because their deeds were evil. For everyone practicing evil hates the light and does not come to the light, lest his deeds should be exposed. But he who does the truth comes to the light, that his deeds may be clearly seen, that they have been done in God.* (John 3:19–21)

Jesus is the Light of the world. (See John 1:4–5.) He loved mankind. He was kind to them and to their children. He healed people and blessed them, but those in darkness could not comprehend. He was a sign that was spoken against. They crucified Him. They tried to turn off the heavenly light, but after He arose from the grave it grew brighter in the upper room. This is why Jesus tells us in Matthew 13:43 that we shall *"shine forth as the sun in the kingdom of* [our] *Father."* We are supposed to be shining people, with the glory of God radiating out in every direction. Of course, those who love evil and want to dwell in darkness will hide from shining Spirit-filled Christians. We are too bright and too hot for them hiding in their denominations that deny God's miracle-working power.

While writing this chapter, one of our church elders told me that he had visited a farm recently where he found that certain cattle had mysteriously died, and a cow had given birth to a calf but the afterbirth would not come away and the cow was desperately sick. First, he rebuked the spirit of death working among the cattle in the barn; then, he laid hands on the sick cow and prayed for it. The same day, the afterbirth came away, the cow recovered, and the production of milk increased one hundred pounds a day. Why did this happen? Because this elder was a walking miracle. Even the veterinary doctor could do nothing! It took a miracle to heal the cow.

If Jesus was a walking miracle, He wants us also to be the same, for He said, "As I am in the world, so are you." (See 1 John 4:17.) He shone, so He gives us the Holy Spirit to radiate from us His miracle-working power. This is why God is now pouring out His Holy Spirit afresh upon all flesh (cows included) to restore His church and to bless His creation. *"Fear not, O land; be glad and rejoice, for the* LORD *has done marvelous things. Do not be afraid, you beasts of the field"* (Joel 2:21–22).

IF WE WANT TO HELP OUR NEIGHBOR COME TO THE CHRIST OF THE BIBLE, WE MUST BE SUCH A SIGN AND WONDER THAT IT WILL BE QUITE OBVIOUS THAT WE ARE DIFFERENT—IN EVERY RESPECT.

A Christian should be a sign and a wonder among the people. Today, this is so necessary because of the general decline of the average man. He is emotionally and physically sick. He takes alcohol in increasing quantities. He is spending more money on "miracle" drugs. He knows we live in a dangerous age and is therefore trying to escape from the inevitable collapse of this world system, called Babylon or confusion in Scripture. It is to be replaced by the kingdom of God on earth. If we want to help our neighbor come to the Christ of the Bible, we must be such a sign and wonder that it will be quite obvious that we are different—in every respect. We have healthy minds in healthy bodies. We do not spend large sums of money to try to buy health out of a bottle or to escape reality through a bottle. Every time Satan attacks us, we repulse him; we resist him in Jesus's name. We cast him out by force from every situation and maintain a position of strength and health. Again, let me remind you that salvation (*soteria*) means "wholeness." Dr. C. I. Schofield, in the footnotes of his well-known Bible, states that the word *salvation* is the most inclusive word in Scripture. It includes all the redemptive acts of the cross. It includes continuing health up to the time of death, for we read in Psalm 91:16, *"With long life I will satisfy him, and show him My salvation."* The Hebrew word for *"salvation"* is *yeshuah*, which is the root meaning of the Greek *Jesus*. Thus, Jesus is the one who gives us salvation—health, wealth, happiness, forgiveness, ease (in contradistinction to disease), and safety. There are many more things He gives us under the comprehensive word *salvation*! In fact, our personal manifestation of these attributes shows we are walking miracles, because they are not natural to us by our biological birth. These are supernatural manifestations of a risen Savior and are outworked in and through our minds and bodies. First, He comes into our spirits; then, He occupies our minds and bodies. Instead of having psychosomatic sicknesses, we have psychosomatic health. A healthy mind outworks through a healthy body. A soul at ease dwells in a body without disease.

What should our spiritually built-in reaction be when we are attacked in sickness of mind or body? It often begins with a shock! We should immediately call for the pastor or a friend to pray with us. This casts away Satan's cohorts who would want to put a sickness upon us. If we accept the sickness, we become sick. If we reject it in forceful, believing prayer, we put up the covering of the blood of Jesus so that Satan is not able to penetrate. We remain well. The problem, of course, is that sometimes Satan catches us off guard, and before we realize it, he has put a sickness upon us. It is then that the battle begins. We trusted God and now we are sick, and then Satan shouts at us, "Yes, and you trusted a phony Bible." In this day of deliverance, there are uncounted thousands coming for help because their churches have not taught them. They are believers but not walking miracles, and they need the help of those who are. We pray for them, cast the sicknesses and demons out of them, pray for them to be filled with the Holy Spirit, and put them in a position so they also can become walking miracles.

Some Bible colleges and schools actually forbid their students to speak in tongues, to pray for the sick, or to cast out demons, and yet they advertise themselves as Bible colleges! When Jesus walks in their doors in miracle form, through any of their student body, they reject it, thereby rejecting Jesus. It is time for the whole church to be shaken from top to bottom by a return of miracle-working men and women in their midst. The whole creation groans and waits for the manifestation of mature, miracle-working sons of God. This is the time that a great maturing is taking place. It is the time of the outpouring of the latter rain. It is now.

SOME BIBLE COLLEGES AND SCHOOLS
ACTUALLY FORBID THEIR STUDENTS TO SPEAK
IN TONGUES, TO PRAY FOR THE SICK,
OR TO CAST OUT DEMONS, AND YET THEY
ADVERTISE THEMSELVES AS BIBLE COLLEGES!
WHEN JESUS WALKS IN THEIR DOORS IN
MIRACLE FORM, THROUGH ANY OF THEIR
STUDENT BODY, THEY REJECT IT,
THEREBY REJECTING JESUS.

As we read the psalms, we find that the word *praise* is mentioned 165 times in 150 psalms. The whole emphasis is one of praise at all times. *"I will bless the* LORD *at all times"* (Psalm 34:1). In the New Testament, Paul had no doubt about it. Though he was stoned, shipwrecked, and starved, he always praised God, and wrote in Ephesians 5:20, *"Giving thanks always for all things to God."* Again, in 1 Thessalonians 5:18, *"In everything give thanks."* For everything, and in everything. When we get in a mess, we should start thanking God for the mess, because the mess is the way to deliverance. There can be no suffering without its corresponding healing. There can be no problem without its answer of deliverance. As soon as we go into battle, we start singing like the Israelites did of old.

"*He* [Jehoshaphat] *appointed those who should sing to the* LORD...*as they went out before the army and* [said], *Praise the* LORD, *for His mercy endures forever*" (2 Chronicles 20:21). It was when the 120 singers praised God in the newly dedicated temple that the house was filled with the *shekinah* glory of God and the priests could not stand but fell to the ground and the glory of the Lord filled the house of God. (See 2 Chronicles 5:12–15.) Notice too that the exact number of priests is given as 120. This is the number of the miracle-working power of God, for there were 120 initial members of the body of Christ who sounded forth from their lips the praises of God in tongues. They were the fulfillment of 120 silver trumpets, for silver is the metal of redemption, and 120 trumpets represent the miracle-working power of God sounding forth out of their mouths. They became miracle workers. If 120 singers brought down the visible *shekinah* glory of God in the temple under the old covenant, what will 120 Spirit-filled people accomplish in the supernatural realm by praising God together in tongues? No wonder Satan fights tongues.

Great emphasis is being made again today in charismatic circles to praise God for everything and in every situation. It is no exaggeration to teach that this will be the beginning of your deliverance to a life of miracle health. It is your trial that forms the first part of your deliverance. Praise Him for it, for His mercy endures forever.

8

CREATING MIRACLES

Whoever says to this mountain, "Be removed and be cast into the sea," and does not doubt in his heart, but believes that those things he says will be done, he will have whatever he says.
—Mark 11:23

Just before Christmas 1974, my wife and I went shopping in our largest shopping mall. It was a Friday night and it seemed the huge parking lot was crammed full. I circled the perimeter, but no place appeared and other cars were milling around looking for the elusive parking spot. I said to my wife, "Say, 'In the name of Jesus, I create a parking spot.'" She repeated the words somewhat half-heartedly, because I told her to do so. Then, I turned into the middle of the area and every place was full. My wife said, "Let's turn down this lane." "No," I replied, "I feel a leading to go down this one." We approached the entrance to the main shopping center, and as we drove a car backed out of a parking spot nearest to the main entrance. It could not have been nearer, and we slid our car into this place with no waiting.

My wife admitted she was half-hearted in her commanding prayer and not listening too closely for guidance afterward. The point had been proved. We had created a parking spot. Isn't this typical of so many of the small details of our lives? We first give a negative confession. We say, "The parking lot is full; we shall never get in there." Or "I'm too busy today; it will be impossible to do that." "Impossible," did you say? That word is used by Jesus as referring to men. *"With men it is impossible, but not with God; for with God all things are possible"* (Mark 10:27). We try in our own strength and fail. We reason with carnal reasoning and come up with defeat, but the impossible becomes the possible by the command of faith that creates something that does not appear to be there.

Conversely, in the case of the mountain before us, we destroy it by the command of faith and it disappears. To do such a thing is ridiculous to the reasoning mind of man. I well remember a case that almost seems to be stupid. It was in England. I was doing up a parcel and needed some string. We were staying with friends, and they could find no string at all and the stores were closed. Thus, I said, "I command a piece of string to appear." My friend looked up in surprise and said that this was fanatical, I then opened a drawer in his kitchen, and there, lying on top, was just the length of string for the parcel. Did I create it? I don't think so, but my commanding prayer had caused me to open the only drawer in the house where the only piece of string existed. It saved a lot of trouble.

This kind of thing would seem to be a series of coincidences, but to those who use this form of commanding faith it works too often to be coincidence. Our problem is that we think it ridiculous to talk like that who would ever think to command a mountain to disappear!

Long ago, Zerubbabel was rebuilding the foundations of the temple. This is typical of the rebuilding of the church in our day. There were (and are) many difficulties. The people living in the land opposed every move and the builders held the trowel in one hand and the sword in the other. The position grew into mountain-sized proportions until Zerubbabel started talking to the mountain—yes, right out loud. He said, *"Who are you, O great mountain? Before Zerubbabel you shall become a plain!"* (Zechariah 4:7). As the builder began to work, the mountain slowly disappeared and became as flat ground. The building was completed, and so will it be in this last generation, as the Word of the Lord comes again through the lips of His servants, commanding all opposition of Satan to cease, so that the completed church without spot or wrinkle may grow into a holy temple. (See Ephesians 2:21.)

IT IS CLEAR THAT BELIEVERS ARE SUPPOSED TO PERFORM MIRACLES FOR PEOPLE TODAY. HOW? BY FIRST GOING INTO THE UPPER ROOM, RECEIVING THE MIRACLE-WORKING POWER OF THE SPIRIT, AND THEN GOING INTO OUR CHURCHES AND GIVING IT TO THOSE WHO THIRST.

The church in past times has been very timid. It has not had the baptism of the Holy Spirit for power and service, but has relied upon the experience of the rebirth to be sufficient. It has not proceeded from the cross to the upper room. It has wrongly assumed it received the power of the Spirit at the cross and failed to go into the upper room at all until this generation. Now, thousands are climbing the steps and returning speaking in other tongues. The early church did not stay in the upper room, although the religious Jews rudely cried out that they were drunk at nine o'clock in the morning. The church then mingled with the people and immediately demonstrated the miracle of healing the man at the gate Beautiful. As has been said, the beggar asked for alms, but God gave him legs! Peter said, *"What I do have I give you: In the name of Jesus Christ of Nazareth, rise up and walk"* (Acts 3:6). What did Peter have? The *dunamis* miracle of the Holy Spirit, received shortly before in the upper room.

He was able to give this miracle power to the lame man, for had not Jesus said, *"Freely you have received, freely give"* (Matthew 10:8), and Jesus was referring to healing the sick, cleansing the lepers, casting out demons, and raising the dead. It is clear that believers are supposed to perform miracles for people today. How? By first going into the upper room, receiving the miracle-working power of the Spirit, and then going into our churches and giving it to those who thirst.

So many in our classic Pentecostal churches have not realized this tremendous truth. They have received the Spirit and spoken in tongues but have not moved out with the commission of Jesus. Denominations have been built around Acts 2:4 and the gifts of the Spirit were dropped in favor of programs. We must demonstrate these supernatural gifts of the Spirit to those who are emerging from the historical churches today. They must *see* and *hear* the miracles as the people did in Philip's visit to Samaria. (See Acts 8.)

It is for us who have received the baptism in the Spirit to start enforcing the law of love by setting people free instead of letting them remain in bondage in our churches. No, we will not be popular when we start, but a full-gospel Christian is not supposed to be popular! The law of love of Calvary is that Jesus has set the prisoners free. He forgave their sins, healed their sicknesses, and delivered them from their satanic oppressions.

I heard recently of a learned pastor of an old-line denominational church who wrote an article for publication in some erudite magazine against speaking in tongues. He mailed it to the publisher and then visited a convention that weekend, during which time he received the baptism in the Spirit, speaking in tongues. He immediately wrote another letter instructing the publisher to destroy his previous manuscript. It takes a miracle to change our theology sometimes. When this man had a miracle in his mouth, his very speech changed from negative to positive. What beautiful rectification!

To create a miracle it is better to say than to pray. Of course, in this case saying is praying, but it is creative praying. Jesus did not pray to the

Father to calm the storm; He calmed it by speaking to the forces behind the wind and the waves and they obeyed Him. If He hadn't commanded, they all would have sunk, and where would you and I be if Jesus had drowned? We would have been sunk too!

Zerubbabel said that as he had started the building, he was going to finish the building and nothing, literally nothing, was going to stop him fulfilling the command of God. Are you going to let anything stop the conversion of that son, that daughter, or the recreation of your marriage entered into by solemn covenant with God and man? Are you going to allow that church to collapse in schisms, or your neighborhood to go to the dogs? You and I have it in our power to command what is going to happen. If we are snared by the words of our mouth (see Proverbs 6:2) and bring ourselves into captivity as a frenzied, frustrated beast in a cage, we can likewise open the doors of that cage by speaking words of authority and turn a negative confession to a positive one.

Look around you, and see where you have accepted defeat and bondage, and decide to change your life by doing a bit of commanding for a change. Start off by saying, "I refuse to accept this situation in the name of Jesus, and I command that it shall agree with Scripture. Sickness go and health return." Keep this up until it becomes a self-evident fact. You create your own miracle.

It is hard to find church members who will enter into such a covenant with you. Even if you get them to start praying-saying in this unfamiliar way, they will do so with little faith, rather wondering what people would say if they heard them, or wondering if anything will really happen. Jesus said, "If you do not doubt in your heart." (See Mark 11:23.) This is the real crux of the matter, the touchstone that tests our faith. Can we really say it and believe it will happen? Whether we can or not does not alter the fundamental law given us by Jesus.

Our first approach to any difficulty is usually a rational one. We start thinking and scheming and we add and subtract. We measure the tons of dirt in the mountain with our puny machinery, and we give up. It isn't possible, and every reasonable person will agree with us. Maybe, but not Jesus. He will say, "Have you tried commanding?" No, we have not. "Well, will you start today?"

I am sure that the reason that few believe in miracles today is that they have not expected them. They had no idea how to create them, and so modern civilization has crawled into a rational cave called "Cave Despair." We expect to get ourselves out of every mess by self-help and psychology. Pride will not allow us to ask Jesus to help. Jesus says, "Take my name and the authority vested in you to do the same works that I did on earth and make it work." This is how the seventy acted. (See Luke 10:19.) *"Even the demons are subject to us in Your name"* (Luke 10:17). Yes, but they had to command the demons! They had to speak out loud; then they saw the miracles.

In Luke 9:43–44, we read that the people were amazed at the mighty power of God and wondered at the miracles that Jesus did; then He said, *"Let these words sink down into your ears"* (verse 44). Our trouble is that we are so taken up with our problems (and other people's), with television and other mind-drugging recreations that the sayings of Jesus accompanied by His miracles fail to reach our minds at all. I think it most striking that Jesus should have used such words as *"sink down."* Do we give time today in our hurried world to allow His words to sink down deep into our consciousness?

OUR TROUBLE IS THAT WE ARE SO TAKEN UP
WITH OUR PROBLEMS (AND OTHER PEOPLE'S),
WITH TELEVISION AND OTHER MIND-DRUGGING
RECREATIONS THAT THE SAYINGS OF JESUS
ACCOMPANIED BY HIS MIRACLES FAIL TO
REACH OUR MINDS AT ALL.

The disciples failed to understand what Jesus was talking about and they were afraid to ask Him. Isn't this true of us today? It takes a marvelous miracle of speaking in tongues to pull us out of our troubles and put us on new faith ground, where we can know the will of God and we can enforce it by commanding and believing. We *shall have* whatsoever we say. Go on, I dare you to say it!

This teaching need not amaze people. The Bible clearly teaches that a full-gospel Christian is *in Christ*. We operate in Him and not outside of Him. He is our strength and intelligence and we have the mind of Christ. (See 1 Corinthians 2:16.) We may not always use His mind within us, but we have it! This has been our trouble. We have not used what He has given us—His authority, His power, and His mind. Without wishing to appear irreverent, He is the ultimate Boss. He is so great that He is the King of kings and the supreme Potentate of all time. And we are *in Him*. He is *in us*. So, when we start acting as if we are the boss (in Him), the devil must give way to the Boss's voice. We roar like the Lion of Judah. We give the commands and woe unto Satan if he obeys not our commands.

Know the Bible and your authority first. Doubt not in your heart, and start taking the position of the officer in command and not the slave under the lash.

9

FALSE MIRACLES

For they are spirits of demons, performing signs.
—Revelation 16:14

Not everything that glitters is gold; neither is every apparent miracle of God. Many become perplexed when they are told that supernatural things can happen apart from God.

This Scripture above describes the conditions of the world in which we live today. The work of these demons, whom Young describes as "deified spirits," that is, evil spirits that are worshipped as gods, are sent forth into the world for one express purpose, to bring the kings of the earth down to Armageddon for judgment. Their work is to deceive by miracles. Always remembering our definition that a miracle is an act that transcends the understanding or ability of man, these powerful demons, often called "familiar spirits," because they are familiar to the mediums through whom they operate, work behind the scenes of all occult groups to deceive. Just before the battle of Armageddon, it seems their activity greatly increases to the point where Satan worship, spiritism, and witchcraft become extremely common. This is certainly true in our generation.

When the Bible was taken out of American schools by a foolish Supreme Court, and prayers in the name of Jesus were forbidden, Satan immediately brought witchcraft into every school in the United States. The true religion of Jesus Christ, God's Son, and the Holy Spirit was replaced by the false religion of Satan and his demons. The Holy Spirit's generous powers were replaced by the debilitating powers of unholy spirits. If there is a spiritual vacuum, Satan will fill it with demons. They desire to be worshipped, so they get into young girls in high schools who become the oracles, or witches, of their peers. Fortune telling becomes the name of the game, and then courses are held in "parapsychology" in some of our universities to study and examine the "scientific" basis of the supernatural and the unknown. Subjects such as levitation, bending of metals, breaking of concrete slabs, and the disappearance of objects, the making of holes through walls and the catapulting of people out of bed, etc., are studied for a scientific basis. These are genuine miracles, for they transcend the understanding of man. They are false miracles, for they do not glorify God.

These are pointless miracles, unless one understands them in the entertainment sense. They do not glorify Jesus. Demons bend metals in front of television cameras. Men and objects can sail into the air as transported by invisible demons. Evil spirits can take an object and carry it out of the room so quickly that it becomes demonic sleight of hand. There is nothing new in these things, but great attention is now being drawn to them, for they are happening all over the world because of the great increase of interest in the occult.

If a heathen prays to an idol in a heathen temple, there is a demon who operates through that idol and may actually come right inside it when candles are lit and incense burned (or joss sticks). The spirit will endeavor to answer prayers, sometimes spectacularly, so that the person will believe that either God Himself or some great, powerful deity is ready to answer their prayers. This principle is known by witch doctors in Africa and Asia who have fetishes, or images of their gods in picture form or in bodily form. These are often hung round necks or put round the necks of cattle or children for protection! Each of these replicas will entice the demon who serves the idol or picture. He works through this system. Witch doctors can cause death in a person by sending an evil spirit of death to kill. They are sent after the prayers and oblations are made to the false god. Destruction of crops can occur, but the witch doctor will charge heavily for his services. How different to the prayers made in Jesus's name for healing or blessing upon an individual. No charge!

The whole business of inquiring of the dead that occurs in spiritist séances is called necromancy and is expressly forbidden in Scripture (see Deuteronomy 18:9–11); in fact, there is absolutely no statement in Holy Writ that a human living on earth may communicate by prayer or supplication with any departed person, saint or sinner, whether in heaven or hell. The only one with whom we may communicate is the Lord Jesus Christ Himself, and the means whereby we do this is the Holy Spirit. Caution must be urged about the practice of praying to dead people, so expressly forbidden, because if we do communicate with someone on the "other end" it may well be a simulating evil spirit. There is only one Mediator between God and man, and His name is Jesus. (See 1 Timothy 2:5.) Absolutely none other.

SATAN, THROUGH HIS ANGELS, WILL ALWAYS CORRUPT. HE WILL ALWAYS CAUSE MEN TO EXERCISE VIOLENCE TOWARD EACH OTHER, INDIVIDUALLY AND NATIONALLY.

In Genesis 6:11–12, we see a description of the world in Noah's day. It is described as being corrupt and filled with violence—an apt picture of modern (so-called) civilization. God told Noah He would destroy the earth and all mankind. Who made them corrupt? None other than Beelzebub, the Lord of the flies, and of all corruption upon the earth. Satan, through his angels, will always corrupt. He will always cause men to exercise violence toward each other, individually and nationally.

Jesus told us that the world before His coming would be as in Noah's day. (See Matthew 24:37–39.) The world system is up for judgment. It is called Babylon or confusion, and its primary contents are political, financial, and ecclesiastical. The three spirits like frogs (see Revelation 16:13) are behind these systems, which are now disintegrating as we watch the hand of God at work restoring the true church. Satan and his demons are doing their best to cause as much confusion as possible today, for they know their time is short: *"Woe to the inhabitants of the earth and the sea! For the devil has come down to you, having great wrath, because he knows that he has a short time"* (Revelation 12:12). This time is also described by Jesus—*"On the earth distress of nations, with perplexity"* (Luke 21:25). There is no way out. God has trapped man in a corner, and when he sees there is no way out he will cry to God. Politics, money, and a backslidden church will be unable to help him. This is the day of the unparalleled demon activity. We should also remember that Jesus said that it would also be as in the time of Sodom and Gomorrah, which were destroyed by fire and earthquake, so that the exact location under the Dead Sea is unknown. (See Luke 17:28–30.) Satan knows his time is short, so he is bringing his harvest of tares to maturity while Jesus is bringing His church to maturity for His coming. Both these harvests are being prepared by miracles, the true and the false.

It is interesting to note that when Jesus told His disciples that they had power (*exousia*—authority) over all the power of the enemy (see Luke 10:19), the word used for Satan's power here is *dunamis*, which, as we have already explained, means miracle power. This verse, therefore, means that all Christians have authority over the very miracle-working power of Satan. He does work miracles!

One of the best cases that comes to mind is the British healer named Harry Edwards. He makes no apology for explaining that he heals "by the spirits," not the Holy Spirit as in the case of true divine healing and the working of miracles. He can pack the Royal Albert Hall in London with seven thousand people and they will witness miracles done by demons. Many that attend believe all this is of God.

It should be explained that, in case of healing by occult spirits, Satan does not cast out Satan, for that would mean his house would be divided against itself. (See Matthew 12:26.) If it brings glory to the devil he will temporarily take away a spirit of infirmity so that sick persons will believe they have been healed by God, while yet in an unregenerative state, and thus the apparent healing will not keep them out of hell. In many cases the spirit is actually driven deeper into the soul of the sufferer, and ultimately they may suffer some strong emotional problems. They are not delivered in the sense that the evil spirit is cast out by force in Jesus's name; they have a temporary easement as the indwelling evil spirit changes positions. To go to an occult healer is a sufficient reason to end up in a worse state than at the beginning.

I corresponded with a spiritist medium by tape some years ago, and he explained to me that he healed with the help of the angels, and he was right, but they are fallen angels. Jesus makes this clear to us in telling us why God created hell, which is a mystery to so many. Here are His words: *"Depart from Me,…into the everlasting fire prepared for the devil and **his angels**"* (Matthew 25:41). Hell was not made for man, but if man insists on doing business with Satan, he will have to accompany him there, with all his angels. Yes, Satan has angels, messengers, evil personalities who fell from heaven in their first rebellion. (See Revelation 12:7–9.) There has to be some place to dump all these terrible evil spirits that are even now trying to destroy society and everything therein. This is why the Greek work *Gehenna* is taken from the Valley of Hinnon, the old rubbish dump outside Jerusalem, where everything from rotting vegetation to dead animal carcasses was burned and the odor was terrible. Flies everywhere, and Satan was lord of them.

It is these angels that work with spiritist mediums. When the mediums go into trances, the demons take over control of the human by his desire and intention. The voices and the healing miracles that follow are done by the demons through the medium, even as healings are done by Jesus indwelling the believer when he prays. The one is the converse of the other. How nice it sounds in the ear of a gullible Christian who doesn't know his Bible, to be told that he can go to a sanctuary and receive prayer from a man (or woman) healer who will lay hands on, probably rub his hands on, the sufferer and the angels will help in the healing. Beautiful, isn't it? No, it's diabolical! Healings are not the only miracles, however. In a séance, all kinds of different colored lights can appear, trumpets can sail round the room and objects move through the air. Horrible odors can be detected and the demons will talk either through the medium or through trumpets. But why advertise the devil and his miracle-working power? Only to warn the unwary.

IF ONLY THE CHURCH IN PAST GENERATIONS HAD WORKED TRUE MIRACLES BY THE POWER OF THE HOLY SPIRIT AND HONORING OF THE BLOOD OF JESUS, SATAN WOULD HAVE HAD MUCH GREATER DIFFICULTY IN GETTING HIS SHOW ON THE ROAD. A LARGE SECTION OF THE CHRISTIAN CHURCH HAS DENIED THE POWER OF GOD AND NOT EXPECTED ANY MIRACLES AND HAS TAUGHT PEOPLE THAT THE DAY OF MIRACLES HAS PASSED.

If only the church in past generations had worked true miracles by the power of the Holy Spirit and honoring of the blood of Jesus, Satan would have had much greater difficulty in getting his show on the road. A large section of the Christian church has denied the power of God and not expected any miracles. It has taught people that the day of miracles has passed. While they are saying this, the day of miracles is rapidly reappearing for them to see. Bishop Pike tried to communicate with his son. He believed in the supernatural, but the very god he sought after destroyed him in the desert of Israel. The bishop was a member of the church, and it must be said with sorrow, that some of these old-line churches that deny the reality of miracles of God today will excuse anyone seeking after the false miracles of Satan, for it is taught by them that this proves the "afterlife." It does nothing of the sort. It proves the existence of the world of spirits behind the natural sight of man.

The reality of the afterlife is only to be accepted on faith by reading the Word of God. Jesus demonstrates the reality of the world beyond our world by baptizing us in the Holy Spirit, bringing us the miracle of tongues. That should prove everything for those who want proof.

In Revelation, chapter 13, reference is made to another beast, who comes up out of the earth. He does great wonders (*semeion*) and deceives mankind by the miracles (*semeion*) that he had power to do before men. The first beast in Revelation 13:2 was given power (*dunamis*) by the dragon, so these two beast systems, which many believe were the successive Babylonian empires with their false religions, right up to recent times, were actually operated by strong demonic powers, and they were backed up by false miracles in their religious systems. The only trouble for the devil is that after he has exercised great power and authority among nations, God finally finishes him and locks him up, whereas Jesus is the Alpha and Omega, having neither beginning nor ending. His miracles stand for all time.

Do not go to soothsayers and astrologers to know the future.

Go to the Bible and pray for the Holy Spirit to give you understanding. If you need salvation in any aspect, go to Jesus; bare your soul and ask His forgiveness and ask Him to save you and fill you with His Spirit. You will be satisfied with His miracles after that.

Expect a miracle every day.

10

SPONTANEOUS MIRACLES

Without shedding of blood is no remission.
—Hebrews 9:22

Perhaps some of the most spectacular and exciting miracles are those that happen when people least expect them. The medical profession refer to these cases as "remissions" and, of course, though many of the medical doctors may not realize it, the Word of God teaches us that *"without shedding of blood is no remission"* (Hebrews 9:22). Because Jesus shed His blood for all mankind, it is possible for people to have a remission from their sickness or killing disease. There is no question that in the Western world, many will pray for someone who is grievously sick. This is especially true among our churches. Prayer requests are sent in and congregational prayer is made, or the request is passed to groups who exist especially for this ministry. How can we understand the love of God in bringing remission to someone who is not even aware that others far off and unknown may be praying for their healing? We cannot limit the hand of God in reaching down from heaven and "sending away" a sickness because Jesus shed His blood for all mankind. The expression "sending away" is the exact meaning of the word *"remission"* (in Greek, *aphesis*).

We remember the time when the well-known Congo missionary W. F. Burton, of the Congo Evangelistic Band, was dying of cancer in Congo. A woman in Melbourne, Australia, was awakened at 3 AM local time to pray for Rev. Burton, who was in dire need.

She obeyed the prompting of the Spirit and interceded for this missionary. At that exact moment of time, Willie Burton had a remission of his cancer. He published a photograph of his cancerous colon before and after this miracle. It was a spontaneous remission. It was a long time later that the truth was learned. Melbourne and the Congo jungles are a long way apart. Distance is nothing to God.

In our own church, we have often been amazed at the testimonies that have later been reported to us by people for whom we prayed in our regular services. We probably did not even know them, but their case was reported to us, and usually before our opening time of prayer, we ask for spoken and unspoken prayer requests. We do not do this as a form, for experience has shown us that spontaneous remissions do take place in many cases. Of course, I do not even attempt to explain why some are not healed, but I suspect it may have something to do with the attitude toward God of the unknown person being prayed for. Not only are many sicknesses spontaneously healed, but it seems that a Spirit-filled Christian will "automatically" react to another person's need. The Spirit in us seems to be most anxious to rise to the help of the person who is stricken, and before we realize it, we are praying for them. Many times, when an aircraft flies over, I find myself praying for the safe journey of those in the air. Is this a kind of superstition for the ignorant, or is it a God-given attribute? I think there is a connection here in Romans 8:26:

> *Likewise the Spirit also helps in our weaknesses. For we do not know what we should pray for as we ought, but the Spirit Himself makes intercession for us with groanings which cannot be uttered.*

The Amplified Bible puts it this way: *"The Spirit Himself goes to meet our supplication and pleads in our behalf with unspeakable yearnings and groanings too deep for utterance."* *The Living Bible* translates this: *"The Holy Spirit prays for us with such feeling that it cannot be expressed in words."*

Here we have a fact revealed. The Holy Spirit (not us) intercedes, prays, pleads, and goes to meet us in our desperate need. This is a spontaneous act of a loving God to start in motion a process to bring a miraculous remission to a person groaning in need. How wonderful that this ministry is inbuilt in the Spirit-filled church!

How do we know how many people may have prayed for one sufferer? How do we know how many people God may have urged to pray in distant lands? Suddenly a person is healed, and it is called a remission. Blood for blood. Jesus's pure, clean, precious blood for our sick, defiled blood. Remission.

The amazing ministry of Kathryn Kuhlman has proved this point beyond any further doubt. I was speaking to one of the leaders of the Catholic healing ministry, Father Francis McNutt, and he explained that thousands of Catholics went seeking healing and remission in her meetings, and thousands of them found health. Miss Kuhlman's large healing services were in no sense a shrine. She happened to be a prophetess. She did not claim to be an evangelist or a preacher. She was certainly no healer. We leave that word to the metaphysicians, but she established a ministry where Jesus was honored through the omnipresent Holy Spirit, and people from all denominations came, hoping or believing they would receive healing. Doctors were present to confirm these healings.

How do spontaneous remissions occur in such services (because they do!)? The answer must be found in the fact that the whole auditorium is charged with the presence of the Holy Spirit. The service is conducted in such a way as to cause people to expect the Holy Spirit to work. These healings are the sovereign work of God. If a dead battery comes in contact with a live battery, the life in the fully charged cells goes into the dead cells. So it is in the case of the cells of the human body. The presence of disease means there are many sick cells, run-down cells, and exhausted cells. They need a new charge of divine life. By moving into an auditorium that has been prayed over, sung over, rejoiced over, and the blood of Jesus honored, tired cells in weary, sick people begin to experience a new charge of *zoe* life from God by the Holy Spirit. The presence of the Holy Spirit will send away—remit—the sickness as a new infusion of divine life flows into the body. Remember that when God created man in His own image, He did so by breathing His divine breath into the lifeless body of Adam, who thereupon became a living soul. (See Genesis 2:7.) All the cells of Adam's perfectly formed body were good cells, but they were all dead cells. It took the breathing of *ruach* (Hebrew for breath) to bring full life and strength to Adam. All of us are descended lineally from Adam and Eve, so when our cells are attacked by Satan with disease, there is a force far greater than the devil and sickness that can drive out disease, namely the very breath of God, strongly present in these Kuhlman healing services.

THE PRESENCE OF THE HOLY SPIRIT WILL SEND AWAY—REMIT—THE SICKNESS AS A NEW INFUSION OF DIVINE LIFE FLOWS INTO THE BODY. REMEMBER THAT WHEN GOD CREATED MAN IN HIS OWN IMAGE, HE DID SO BY BREATHING HIS DIVINE BREATH INTO THE LIFELESS BODY OF ADAM, WHO THEREUPON BECAME A LIVING SOUL.

If you put a damp, rotting object in a warm oven, the process of degeneration and decay temporarily ceases as the object is dried out.

Where a sick person exposes himself to the warmth of the Holy Spirit this "drying out" process begins to take place. After the decay has been arrested in the cells of the body, the restorative processes already resident in the bodily cells begin to take over, and with a supercharged "shot" of the Holy Spirit, healing may take place very quickly. This is a spontaneous remission.

Symbols of the Holy Spirit are fire, which cauterizes; water, which cleanses away dirt; breath, which revives and resuscitates; and oil, which soothes. All these represent the work of the Holy Spirit in a public meeting hall or church where Jesus is honored as Healer and His blood honored as a life restorer. Kathryn Kuhlman often said publicly that she could not understand why miracles took place in her meetings, for not all people who went had faith. Even if a person is compelled to go by a loving wife, husband, child, or friend, the fact that they go is, in itself, an indication of faith, however small. The fact that loved ones, who almost compel the sufferer to go, are all praying, is reason for a miracle of spontaneous remission to take place. We are not always healed solely on our own faith; in fact, in deep distress and sickness, it might be very difficult indeed for the sufferer to exercise faith at all. The fact that they come brings them into the power-charged presence of the Holy Spirit Himself, who intercedes for us. Try to imagine a large healing service in which there are many poor, suffering people. Most of the people present are in an attitude of prayer, and this causes a spontaneous pleading by the Holy Spirit to the Father to release His life-giving breath to all. People in wheelchairs who have been unable to gain access into the main auditorium are healed in the outside passages, or even outside the building. It is sudden, it is spontaneous, it is a miracle, but it is Jesus who creates the remission.

As the church is increasingly restored by the Holy Spirit in the days in which we live, we shall see much more of this mass healing. In the Old Testament the priests were not able to stand to minister after the blood was offered, because the temple area was filled with a visible glory cloud. *"The house of the LORD, was filled with a cloud, so that the priests could not continue ministering because of the cloud; for the glory of the* LORD *filled the house of God"* (2 Chronicles 5:13–14).

In Kathryn Kuhlman's meetings, many people fell to the ground, either when touched or simply in her presence. Many have queried this unusual manifestation, for admittedly it does not happen in many churches; but spontaneous remissions do not happen in many churches either, which is why people flocked to Miss Kuhlman's meetings seeking their healing. It seems that the falling to the ground may be a New Testament fulfillment of what happened in the Old Testament temple. The glory of God was present and, as it is recorded in Luke 5:16–17, Jesus withdrew into the wilderness to pray. Afterward, He returned and started to teach doctors of the law who had gathered out of every town in Galilee, Judaea, and Jerusalem. It is recorded that in this unusual instruction class, the power (*dunamis*) of the Lord was present to heal. The fact that Jesus Himself was there, and that He was teaching the Word of God, created a situation in which any one of those learned doctors could have received a spontaneous miracle from the miracle-working power of the present Spirit.

When we have the same conditions today, we get the same results. When Spirit-filled men or women dare to get up and pronounce that Jesus is present to heal, the very air becomes charged with the healing virtue of God, and going into such a building, it is not surprising that many do get healed.

WHEN SPIRIT-FILLED MEN OR WOMEN DARE TO GET UP AND PRONOUNCE THAT JESUS IS PRESENT TO HEAL, THE VERY AIR BECOMES CHARGED WITH THE HEALING VIRTUE OF GOD, AND GOING INTO SUCH A BUILDING, IT IS NOT SURPRISING THAT MANY DO GET HEALED.

I mention Kathryn Kuhlman, but there are others today with similar ministries, and these are proliferating, but the gifts of the Holy Spirit revealed to her with perfect accuracy the individuals who were, at that moment, being healed, and the sickness from which they were receiving remissions, showing the presence of the Holy Spirit in a vital way. This happened all over the auditorium, and then, with the help of ushers, those healed were encouraged to come to the platform and testify. It was then that many fell to the ground under the power of God. Let it not be said they were "slain of the Lord," for this expression is reserved for the enemies of God. (See Jeremiah 25:33; Isaiah 66:16.) We sometimes get our expressions a bit mixed up! Those coming into the strong presence of the Holy Spirit, who is honoring the evangelist, simply fall to the ground. They are not healed because they fall; they just fall! The priests in Chronicles could not stand in the presence of the glory cloud—the *shekinah* of God. They were not slain!

We can see the day coming when people will not only fall before the glory of God, but many may fall before they get into the church or public auditorium! In 2 Chronicles 7:1–2, we read:

> When Solomon had finished praying, fire came down from heaven and consumed the burnt offering and the sacrifices; and the glory of the LORD filled the temple. And the priests could not enter the house of the LORD, because the glory of the LORD had filled the LORD's house.

In the same way as many were healed just by passing by the shadow of Peter, so likewise many will be healed in the cities where divine healing services are held. Many sick people lying in hospitals and homes in these cities will suddenly come under the beneficent power of the Holy Spirit and will receive spontaneous remissions. The power of God will so greatly increase in the great restoration and renewal of the church that a saturation point will be created inside the church auditorium, and it will be so great that people will fall before the Lord in streets and on the steps of the building. The power of the Lord will be present to heal in a citywide sense.

These will be very exciting days. Remember the Scripture I quoted: *"Then a great multitude followed Him, because they saw His signs which He performed on those who were diseased"* (John 6:2). Imagine what will happen in some of our modern cities when people actually fall down under the power of God and are spontaneously healed right on the sidewalks! Imagine the crowd of press reporters and TV cameramen who will quickly converge on such a scene, and afterward, the publicity and the pictures, so that multitudes will see and believe on the Son of God. No wonder Kathryn Kuhlman was always saying, "I don't heal anybody!" These healings are from Jesus, by the presence of the Holy Spirit saturating the auditorium. The only way to get our generation out of the impossible conditions of crime and debauchery that prevail is for signs and miracles to take place on a large scale. Then people will follow Jesus, not politicians and celebrities!

11

THE NEW BIRTH

Wash your heart from wickedness, that you may be saved.
—Jeremiah 4:14

If there are degrees of intensity of miracles, and it seems there are, then the rebirth of a person's whole nature is a great miracle. The changing and cleansing of the human heart is a spiritual-surgical operation that would be impossible by the skill of man. As we shall see in this chapter, Jesus, the Great Physician, actually takes our heart out, washes it, and puts it back again an entirely new heart.

Jeremiah knew something of the essential wickedness of the human heart. He wrote, "*The heart is deceitful above all things, and desperately wicked; who can know it?*" (Jeremiah 17:9). Young's Literal Translation is interesting: "*Crooked is the heart above all things, and it is incurable—who doth know it?*" We see, therefore, that the very generator of our lives, that great pump of the heart, is a crooked, off-center thing; its nature is wickedness and there is absolutely no natural cure for its state. It can only continue to pump pollution throughout the mind and body of man unless there is a radical operation.

Jesus leaves us in no doubt as to what this pump will do to us:

But those things which proceed out of the mouth come from the heart, and they defile a man. For out of the heart proceed evil thoughts, murders, adulteries, fornications, thefts, false witness, blasphemies. These are the things which defile a man, but to eat with unwashed hands does not defile a man. (Matthew 15:18–20)

The mouth is the orifice from which the pump of the heart pressurizes all kinds of filthy talk and behavior. Man cannot help it. He has always been like that since Adam was cast out of Eden. He is a fallen creature and a pathetic one. The very motivating power of our lives is the heart; without this life-giving organ we would be dead, and yet it goes on pumping its garbage through our bloodstream. Is there any hope for us? We can understand what Paul had in mind when he wrote, *"O wretched man that I am! Who will deliver me from this body of death?"* (Romans 7:24). Paul knew the answer: *"I thank God—through Jesus Christ our Lord!"* (verse 25). He is the only answer; He must do the divine operation.

Unfortunately, so many wait so long before they apply for this radical operation. They try every means to ignore the impurity which is wrecking their marriage, their job, and their life. They are indeed living in a body of death. We have no chance; the heart goes on pumping, pumping, pumping death into our bloodstream. We cannot get away from this death. We are trapped by a monster—Satan. As a male child is supposed to have its foreskin circumcised on the eighth day of its life, so we also are supposed to have our heart circumcised as soon as possible. The sooner the better, if we are to escape the dangerous actions of the heart, especially when we approach puberty.

Paul understood the mystery of this great operation. He expressed it in Colossians 2:10–12:

And you are complete in Him [Jesus].... In Him you were also circumcised with the circumcision made without hands, by putting

*off the body of the sins of the flesh, by the circumcision of Christ…
through faith in* **the working of God.**

In recent decades, man has learned how to transplant a human
heart. This is an outstanding medical technique, for the old, diseased
heart is cut right out, the arteries carrying the blood are severed, and
the old heart is removed and thrown away; in its place, a healthy heart
from a recently dead person is quickly put into place. All the arteries
are sutured and the blood is again allowed to flow. This is equivalent to
the change of a motor in an automobile. Some have lived for a number
of years with a new heart. To Bible students, this thought reminds us
of David's cry: *"Create in me a clean heart, O God"* (Psalm 51:10). The
Lord promised it to Israel and to all in New Testament Israel—*"I will
give you a new heart…I will take the heart of stone out of your flesh and
give you a heart of flesh"* (Ezekiel 36:26). This radical operation of God
can only be done by His Son, Jesus. First, we must place our bodies on
the altar as a living sacrifice. (See Romans 12:1.) We must trust our
whole lives to Him, knowing that He has the power to bring life out
of death. We must be prepared to die, for obviously if we receive a true
circumcision (cutting round) of our heart and then it is removed, we
die. This is what Paul meant when, writing to the Colossians, he said,
"For you died, and your life is hidden with Christ in God" (Colossians 3:3).
Jesus takes the scalpel of the Word of God, which is sharper than any
earthly instrument, and as we lie on the operating table of the altar of
God, He neatly inserts His knife, the sword of the Spirit, does a quick
360-degree turn, as all the vessels to our heart are severed. Then He
takes our old sinful, dirty, crooked, and wicked heart and cleanses it in
the most concentrated disinfectant in the universe, the blood of Christ.
In Joel 3:21, the Lord promises, *"For I will cleanse their blood that I have
not cleansed"* (KJV).

Once the blood has been applied by sprinkling from the hand of
Jesus, our evil conscience is removed (see Hebrews 10:22), and now
our heart is ready to put back into our body again, for all the old filth
and garbage has been destroyed. I always remember my childhood in

England when the garbage man would sprinkle carbolic powder into the bottom of our garbage containers, as a service from the city! It smelled very nice and effectively destroyed the corruption in the can. A dirty garbage can smells horrible, and so does a dirty heart, for the author of all corruption is Beelzebub, the lord of the flies from the manure pile; but the author of cleansing is Jesus, who sprinkles His blood on our dirty heart. Suddenly the motor is cleansed. The body of death has been delivered, for now a *new heart* is put back, miraculously sutured without a trace of surgery, and the blood of our bodies becomes cleansed by this disinfectant. The body of death becomes the body of life. We are now walking in *"newness of life"* (Romans 6:4). We are those who are alive from the dead. (See Romans 6:13.) We died because our old heart was taken out. We live because a new one has been put back on. This is God's great operation, and now the new heart pumps cleansed, life-giving blood throughout our bodies, bringing spiritual and physical health. This great miracle is the root cause of our obtaining divine health.

THE VERY DECEITFUL HEART OF MAN DEVISES RELIGIOUS SYSTEMS THAT PUT THE WORSHIPPERS INTO A SPIRITUAL SLUMBER, SO THAT THEY NO LONGER ARE ABLE TO COMPREHEND THE WAY OF SALVATION OR THE NEED OF IT. THEY EXPLAIN AWAY THEIR WEAKNESSES AND MISTAKES TO THE WEAKNESS INHERENT IN ALL MANKIND; THIS THEY DESCRIBE AS "HUMAN NATURE."

Within a very short time after I had this radical spiritual operation, my language changed. My mouth became filled with praise instead of swearing and off-color jokes. Any desire for liquor instantly disappeared, and my binding habit of tobacco smoking was miraculously broken when I prayed by myself in all simplicity. I suddenly felt the unclean habit literally lifted off me like being freed from a smothering sack. This was a miracle. The renewed heart no longer had any evil things to pump into my brain, and so a corresponding change naturally occurred in my body, which now obeyed my new heart, and a complete transformation of character took place. The first one to notice this change was my wife, and later she also found Jesus Christ as her Savior and the One who baptized her in the Holy Spirit, and then she found herself a stranger in her church! No one ever spoke of the rebirth in most of the staid Church of England. I was a member of a Calvinist Presbyterian Church, but I had never heard anything about a radical surgical change in the heart.

Isn't it amazing that forms of religion can be developed around the old, unclean heart in the body of death! The very deceitful heart of man devises religious systems that put the worshippers into a spiritual slumber, so that they no longer are able to comprehend the way of salvation or the need of it. They explain away their weaknesses and mistakes to the weakness inherent in all mankind; this they describe as "human nature." They are right, but human nature can be changed to the divine nature. Peter knew it and wrote, *"By which have been given to us exceedingly great and precious promises, that through these you may be **partakers of the divine nature**, having escaped the corruption that is in the world through lust"* (2 Peter 1:4). To partake of this divine nature, we must have a cleansed heart and a new Spirit; this Spirit is the Spirit of Christ, and now, instead of our old heart pumping satanic filth, the renewed heart circulates the very nature of Jesus Christ throughout our veins.

We are taught in the Bible a divine principle: our life is in our bloodstream. (See Leviticus 17:11.) This would seem to indicate that our blood carries the inherited sin of our forefathers. We cannot help being sinners. We are born with the corruption of Adam in our blood. We realize that such Bible teaching is totally abhorrent to those who go their own way, but how else are we to explain the continual appalling behavior of our fellow man? Today, crime in America has reached an all-time high. At the time of this writing, the American police forces feel that crime has overtaken them. This is the only way that people in the United States and other "free" nations will be forced to cry to God for help, and His help can only come by Jesus performing the surgical operation of renewing the hearts of individuals. It is my prayer that God will change the hearts of our leaders. We are commanded to pray for them:

> *I exhort first of all that supplications, prayers, intercessions, and giving of thanks be made for all men, for kings and all who are in authority…. For this is good…in the sight of God our Savior, who desires all men to be saved.* (1 Timothy 2:1–4)

If all the rulers of the free world were to have a true experience of the rebirth, it would transform the planet within weeks.

In the Welsh Revival of 1904–06, sin largely disappeared. The police had nothing to do. The public houses closed down; the theaters had no patrons. This can happen again, and I believe it is beginning to happen in this great charismatic restoration of the church.

The renewal of the heart of the believer will be followed by the renewal of the body in health in this life, and ultimately result in a *"house not made with hands, eternal in the heavens"* (2 Corinthians 5:1)—an everlasting body! One miracle follows another. There is no limit to the number or quality of miracles that will daily occur in the life of one who has received the rebirth. In fact, as we have already shown, our very lives themselves become walking miracles. What a marvelous promise in these days of inflation and depression: *"My God shall supply all your need according to His riches in glory by Christ Jesus"* (Philippians 4:19). There is no inflation or lack in heaven—just a steady flow of blessing, healing, and daily supply from an inexhaustible storehouse.

Jesus promised the same thing. *"But seek first the kingdom of God and His righteousness, and all these things shall be added to you"* (Matthew 6:33).

In the days that are ahead of us, before the great day of the return of Jesus, we are going to experience many amazing miracles—special miracles, outstanding wonders that will confound the world. Our daily provision is in itself a daily miracle. Consider the Lord's Prayer when we pray, *"Give us this day our daily bread"* (Matthew 6:11); but this is contingent upon our being willing at all times to forgive those who trespass against us! As we seek to enjoy the Christian life to the full after our heart transformation, we enter into the life of continual miracles. That is why this book is being written.

12

SPECIAL MIRACLES

Now God worked unusual miracles by the hands of Paul.
—Acts 19:11

This is a very interesting verse. It means, in effect, that there are degrees of miracles, or degrees in the intensity of the power or the signs of God. It is difficult enough to convince many people that God can do just one small miracle, but when we come to the realization that there are great or special miracles, we are entering into the area where God wants to attract attention to Himself in an unusual way today in order to break through the prevalent unbelief in a materialistic age.

The meaning in the Greek for the word *"special"* is "not ordinary," that is to say, extraordinary miracles. This is exciting, especially in our day, when it is quite obvious that miracles are increasing in the church.

What was so extraordinary in this nineteenth chapter of Acts? It was a "first." There was no precedent for this action by the apostle Paul. We read, *"So that even handkerchiefs or aprons were brought **from his body** to the sick, and the diseases left them and the evil spirits went out of them"* (verse 12). This Scripture has often been used today with great success, and it has also been abused. We remember a man in the Midwestern part of the United States who used to anoint pieces of cloth with oil and wine. He explained that the oil was a token of the Holy Spirit, and the wine of the blood of Jesus, and for ten cents, he would send these to those who applied for them. It was recommended that the cloth be worn by the sufferer, and after a month or two, it should be sent back with another ten cents, so that it could again be anointed with oil and wine. There is no scriptural precedent for such action, nevertheless, God is able to heal by any means, as long as faith is found.

As we examine this Scripture by trying to read between the lines, we arrive at the conclusion that this was not a hasty decision by those present in Paul's healing ministry. Obviously, sick people, or the aged, could not easily travel distances to be in Paul's meetings. There were no ambulances, taxis, or private cars, but only donkeys and stretcher carriers walking on foot. Even the Virgin Mary traveled on a donkey! The Spirit of God revealed to someone that if the sufferer was agreeable, a piece of their personal clothing could be taken and put upon Paul's body, or put under the laying on of his hands. This apron or handkerchief would then be merely a token, and a point of contact, so that when the sick person received the garment, they would be in exactly the same position as if Paul laid his hands upon them personally. It was really the laying on of Paul's hands by projection over a distance, for there is no distance in the prayer of faith. If there was a precedent for this action, it would have been found among those who touched the garment that Jesus wore: *"And the whole multitude sought to touch Him* [Jesus], *for power* [dunamis] *went* **out from Him** *and healed them all"* (Luke 6:19). The woman dying of hemorrhage (probably cancer), who was declared unclean by Israel's law, broke through the crowd and touched the hem of His garment and was healed, and again, Jesus felt power (*dunamis*) go out of Him. (See Mark 5:30.) In both Scriptures, miracles went out of Him into them!

Because of the miracles that Jesus did among the sick people, *multitudes* followed Him, and Jesus had to move out into the lake because of the crowd pressing upon Him. It is recorded that *"He healed many, so that as many as had afflictions pressed* [rushed] *about Him to* **touch**

Him" (Mark 3:10). This almost developed into a mild mob scene; the people rushed upon Jesus just to touch Him, and when they did they were healed, and each time a *dunamis* miracle went out of Him, bringing health where incipient death reigned in their bodies before. What a ministry!

Some years ago in Congo, Africa, a young native evangelist who had learned his ministry from the men of the early Congo Evangelistic Band prayed for so many hundreds of people, and so many miracles took place, that in the end, he was totally exhausted. He sat upon a stone, but still the crowds seemed unending, pressing him for the laying on of hands. Finally, he said, "All those who sit on this stone on which I am sitting will be healed, just as if I laid my hands upon you." And so the crowd moved forward, each sitting on the stone, and each received his miracle of healing. These were special miracles. Outstanding, extraordinary evidences of God's miracle power. The young evangelist was drained of human strength. This is a very real problem, for with the increasing manifestation of the power of God today in 1979, I personally know what it is to feel all power leave me, and I have to stop, even if there are others to pray for! I remember ministering with Rev. Don Basham in Birmingham, Alabama, among hundreds of needy people, when suddenly, Don said, "I quit," and he walked to his bedroom. I managed to keep going for another ten minutes and then I quit and went to my bedroom! What shall we do with the multitudes who are yet to come in this great revival and restoration of the church, for the days of extraordinary miracles are upon us again!

The answer to this problem will be that we shall use established methods, such as handkerchiefs and aprons, but no doubt, the Spirit of God will open up new methods that He will honor. Oral Roberts has probably prayed for more thousands than most evangelists, and in some cases, was required to lay hands on over two thousand people in one service. He became so emotionally and physically exhausted that he had to walk for an hour or more because he was so strung up that he could not sleep. Today, he finds that television is a better method of reaching the masses, and there is no doubt that both television and radio will play a tremendous part in bringing healing to the masses.

In the final, great outpouring of the Spirit to bring the church back into conformity with the original pattern, we are going to see extraordinary miracles wrought by extraordinary means, unknown in Jesus's day. Remember that He not only told us that we would do the works (or miracles) that He did, but that in this end time, this last generation, we would do "greater works"! What can this mean? I certainly think it refers to greater in the sense of a much larger number of people affected by the healing ministry of Jesus, but I also believe it means that a greater intensity of extraordinary or special miracles will occur. The people who flocked to Jesus in His day to touch Him will be manyfold greater today—all over the world. The gospel in His day was confined to Palestine, but today it is for the whole wide world. *"This gospel…will be preached in all the world as a witness to all the nations"* (Matthew 24:14). Jesus used the word *"witness"* when telling the Jews that they would become witnesses when the Holy Spirit came upon them (see Acts 1:8), and the meaning of this word, from the Greek *martus*, indicates a person who has been martyred, but is risen from the dead. Thus, a true New Testament witness is, in reality, a walking, living miracle, showing in himself that he is as one who is alive from his old dead ways of life in trespasses and sins. He not only is a miracle, but is able to impart miracles to others. This is the gospel of the kingdom that, in these last days, will be presented to the world by a restored church. It is a gospel that is always confirmed by signs following. The preaching precedes the miracle.

In the Scripture, we have taken to explain special miracles, I would ask you to note that reference is made to sicknesses departing and evil spirits going out. I would suggest that the healing of the sick is often accompanied by the departure of evil spirits. We have shown that the casting out of a demon is equated by Jesus with the working of a miracle (see Mark 9:38–39), and in Matthew 8:16–17, the correlation between casting out evil spirits and the healing of the sick is very close. When Jesus sent out the seventy to heal in His name, He did not actually tell them to cast out demons. He said to them, *"Heal the sick there, and say to them, 'The kingdom of God has come near to you'"* (Luke 10:9). This was their commission, and the proof of their preaching would be the evidence or witness of healing for mind and body. As soon as they returned from this evangelistic journey, they exclaimed, *"Even the demons are subject to us in Your name"* (Luke 10:17). Their commission was to heal the sick, but in doing so they obviously cast out demons, and this was before Pentecost. How much more today, with the power of Pentecost returning to the church, shall we heal the sick by the casting out of demons.

A TRUE NEW TESTAMENT WITNESS IS, IN REALITY, A WALKING, LIVING MIRACLE, SHOWING IN HIMSELF THAT HE IS AS ONE WHO IS ALIVE FROM HIS OLD DEAD WAYS OF LIFE IN TRESPASSES AND SINS.
HE NOT ONLY IS A MIRACLE, BUT IS ABLE TO IMPART MIRACLES TO OTHERS.

This method would surely seem to be in line with the original commission given by Jesus to the twelve apostles. He commanded them first to preach, and then to heal and to cast out demons. *"And as you go,* **preach***, saying, 'The kingdom of heaven is at hand.' Heal the sick, cleanse the lepers, raise the dead, cast out demons. Freely you have received, freely give"* (Matthew 10:7–8). The twelve were not commanded to pray that Jesus would heal them, but that they, using His power and authority, should heal the people by laying on of hands and commanding the sicknesses to depart, just as they did when handkerchiefs and aprons were laid on sick people at a distance. The witness or evidence of their preaching, announcing that the kingdom of God was right there at hand, was the obvious evidence of miracles of healing that occurred before their eyes, often with the evidence of evil spirits leaving.

In my own ministry, as I often tell, it was really when I started taking the offensive by rebuking sickness in Jesus's name and commanding it to come out, that I found myself in a new dimension of faith, for demons manifested themselves to our astonishment when we rebuked sickness, and we found experimentally that evil spirits were often the cause behind visible sickness.

Some astonishing miracles are taking place today. I read in the Australian magazine *The Revivalist*, published by my friend Rev. Leo Harris, of the Christian Revival Crusade, Adelaide, that a girl who was always sick stopped growing at the age of twelve. Her health rapidly degenerated until she was confined to a wheelchair, unable to walk because of a form of arthritis in her knees. She was paralyzed in her whole body and unable to drink water except through a baby's drinking bottle. She was in a home for incurables—a sad case indeed. Some of the ministers of the Revival Crusade got interested in her case and began to pray for her and there were some evidences of beginnings of deliverance. Then, one day, she called another friend of mine, Rev. Ian Simpson, who prayed for her. She asked that the cast be taken off her leg and then asked for a glass of water. Her feet had straightened, her legs and spine had straightened, and she found herself able to drink water normally. Her health rapidly improved and she fell in love with a man in the home who had been injured, and who was recovering. They married, and this hopeless cripple with an underdeveloped body of a twelve-year-old gave birth to a perfect baby. An unusual miracle! This was published in the Victoria press.

A few years ago, another woman lying in a wicker-basket bed on wheels in South Wales was prayed for, but no immediate evidence was seen. Her body was weak, emaciated, and very small! As she was praying one day, her body began to change shape; the bones and sinews began to crack audibly; she grew in height; her legs grew, sinews began to develop, and flesh began to come upon her body. In a few minutes, a tremendous miracle had taken place. This was published in the Welsh press, with photographs before and after the miracle. It was published again in the *Voice of Healing* magazine some years ago in Dallas, Texas.

We think of Marjorie Stevens, in Bournemouth, England, who was crippled with multiple sclerosis. She was in a wheelchair and unable to move her body, but rang a little bell with her mouth if she needed attention. She also was prayed for, and no immediate result was seen. One day, the Lord spoke to her and told her the exact day and hour when the miracle would be manifest. She waited for it, and suddenly, at the time given, every joint in her body came back into place. The arthritis left her instantly and she stood and walked. Then she realized that her parents, who were looking after her, would be shocked, so she got back into her chair, rang the bell, at which they came to help her, and she told them what had happened and prepared them for the shock. Then she slowly arose, walked across the room and then walked downstairs to the piano and began playing hymns. Up to that time, both her arms and legs had been totally paralyzed. She then returned to her profession of nursing. After that she also traveled the British Isles telling of this miracle. We were privileged to hear her in Luton, Bedfordshire.

Other equally great miracles are being reported in an increasing way today, and we can certainly look forward to a proliferation of extraordinary miracles by apron, handkerchief, letter, radio broadcast, and live television, where the preacher will rebuke sicknesses and people hearing and seeing will be healed by extraordinary means.

God wrought special miracles. He is still in the same business!

13

NEGATIVE MIRACLES

So great fear came upon all the church....
Yet none of the rest dared join them.
—Acts 5:11, 13

What is a negative miracle? It is an act of God that brings judgment upon the scornful to protect the church from the invasion of wrong spirits. A positive miracle is one that brings blessing to the church by removing sickness, but a negative miracle is one that causes a serious happening to come on those who willingly oppose God's power. The Bible teaches this.

A negative miracle may be spontaneous, but also it can be precipitated by the prayers or counsel of God's servants. God is determined that His settings of apostles, prophets, pastors, evangelists, and teachers are sacred, which is why we read in the Old Testament: *"He permitted no man to do them wrong...saying, "Do not touch My anointed ones, and do My prophets no harm"* (1 Chronicles 16:21–22). As we approach the time of the full restoration of the church with the five ministry gifts, we are going to see a return of the protective confirmatory power of the

Holy Spirit, which will confound the scornful, so that as we read in the early church, *"Yet none of the rest dared join them"* (Acts 5:13), that is, the Spirit-filled, miracle-working church.

In past ages, and especially today, the church has been held in scorn by many in such areas as the medical profession, the press, and the television networks. This is because it has only a form of godliness, with forms, ceremonies, and superstitions, and we are commanded to turn away from such hypocrisy, because it lacks the dynamic, miracle-working power that brings fear into the hearts of the ungodly. The church is supposed to be a giant in our society, inspiring holy fear in those who oppose themselves to the Spirit of God. When the church is sick, it inspires confidence in nobody.

THE CHURCH IS SUPPOSED TO BE A GIANT IN OUR SOCIETY, INSPIRING HOLY FEAR IN THOSE WHO OPPOSE THEMSELVES TO THE SPIRIT OF GOD. WHEN THE CHURCH IS SICK, IT INSPIRES CONFIDENCE IN NOBODY.

When the early church was enjoying pristine power and zeal, there was a man and wife who did not understand that they served a holy God. They thought they could say one thing and do another, and God would not even know their thoughts! Their names were Ananias and Sapphira, and they were so touched by the moving of the Holy Spirit that they felt led to give money to the work of God, which is always a good thing. They sold a field—a piece of real estate. They had promised God and His servants that the church would receive all they obtained for their land. It is quite possible that they obtained more for it than they had anticipated, and so there was an easy temptation to give God only what they thought they would receive, and they decided to keep the rest. Many would think this a fairly harmless thing; God got most of the proceeds of the sale, and He would certainly understand if they kept some for themselves. After all, it was *their land*.

The miracle-working Spirit of God came upon the apostle Peter and told him that this married couple was lying to the Holy Spirit—not to man. To say to Peter, "We will give you the proceeds of this sale and you can use it in God's work," was equivalent to promising God—not Peter. All that Peter did verbally was to remind Ananias of his promise, and he told him that he had actually lied to God! The result of this spoken rebuke and admonition was that Ananias fell down dead. Many have thought that the great apostle killed him, but not so. God took his life, because he had lied to the Holy Spirit in the midst of the beginnings of the greatest and dearest creation of God—the church, His bride. God would not allow His servants to be mocked. God was quick to bring a negative judgmental miracle. His power was revealed.

Three hours later, Sapphira arrived, and said, "What have you done with my husband?"

And Peter answered her, "Tell me whether you sold the land for so much? And she [lying] said, "Yes, for so much." Then Peter said to her, "How is it that you have agreed together to test the Spirit of the Lord? Look, the feet of those who have buried your husband are at the door, and they will carry you out." (Acts 5:8–9)

She immediately fell dead at the apostle's feet. Did Peter kill her? No, but when he spoke with divine authority, knowing that this woman could not escape the same judgment that came on her husband, the Lord carried out the death sentence. It was these two miracles that brought such great fear upon the members of the church, in order to warn them that there could be no lying in their promises to God. As far as the rest of the Jews were concerned, they just moved out of the orbit of such tremendous people with such powerful leaders like Peter. This was a radical operation of God in the early church. We need more radical operations today to cut out the cancers of lying, stealing, and looking upon God almost with contempt. *"Do not be deceived, God is not mocked"* (Galatians 6:7).

It is a serious business to become a full-gospel Christian today. Our vocation is to magnify the Lord Jesus in our lives, to exercise the gifts of the Spirit, and to bring healing and blessing upon our neighbors, even if they are scared of us! Many people have said to me, "I'm scared of you!" especially when they hear and see demons coming out crying with a loud voice!

Another case comes to mind—the story of Elymas the sorcerer. This man was a warlock, a spiritist medium, possessed of demons, and we have a proliferation of them in the world today! He was even known as "Bar-Jesus," which means "son of a Savior." He was an impostor. Nevertheless, he was full of demonic power, and when the deputy of Paphos enquired of Paul and Barnabas about the true Jesus, this demon-possessed man rose up and opposed their ministry and teaching, trying to turn away the deputy from the knowledge of the truth. Satan tried to interfere with God's true servants. Doesn't he try to do this today, and don't we let him get away with it?

> *Then...Paul, filled with the Holy Spirit, looked intently at him and said, "O full of all deceit and all fraud, you **son of the devil**, you enemy of all righteousness, will you not cease perverting the straight ways of the Lord? And now, indeed, the hand of the Lord is upon you, and you shall be blind, not seeing the sun for a time." And **immediately** a dark mist fell on him, and he went around seeking someone to lead him by the hand. Then the proconsul believed, when he saw what had been done, being astonished at the teaching of the Lord.* (Acts 13:9–12)

This is a good way to get souls saved!

Did Paul make him blind? No. The context shows us that Paul had a word of knowledge of God's intention and merely spoke it to the sorcerer. Then it happened, and God made him blind. This is a very illuminating story and full of warning for the rebellious Christian who dabbles in the occult. Paul was full of the Holy Spirit and Elymas was full of the devil, and because Jesus conquered Satan on the cross, it was an uneven contest for the warlock. The word that came out of Elymas's mouth was a perverted word, but that which came out of Paul was a miracle word, and God worked the miracle, not of giving the man sight, as He had done earlier for Paul, but of taking away his sight. A miracle can work both ways! Paul was three days without sight because of his rebellion against God, but afterward, when he obeyed God, he received his sight back again, and was baptized. (See Acts 9:18.) Paul learned his lesson for all time, and maybe we sometimes have to learn the same lesson, the hard way! It is easy to blame the devil for our sicknesses and infirmities, but maybe it might more profitable if we examined ourselves. In Psalm 51, we read of David's searching prayer that all wickedness and uncleanness might be removed from him. David suffered many chastisements of the Lord. Before we take communion, we should pause and examine ourselves. (See 1 Corinthians 11:28.) The blood of Jesus Christ received by faith in the communion cannot wash away our sins if we are opposing a husband, a wife, or children in their search for God. We are in danger. I wonder if Elymas ever got converted and received his sight back? We can only hope so.

———————————————

BEFORE WE TAKE COMMUNION, WE SHOULD PAUSE AND EXAMINE OURSELVES. THE BLOOD OF JESUS CHRIST RECEIVED BY FAITH IN THE COMMUNION CANNOT WASH AWAY OUR SINS IF WE ARE OPPOSING A HUSBAND, A WIFE, OR CHILDREN IN THEIR SEARCH FOR GOD. WE ARE IN DANGER.

———————————————

Perhaps one of the most awe-inspiring abilities of the church is to give a rebellious person over to the devil. Some people's concept of a loving God would reject such a proposition as contrary to their understanding of God. Do we not read God is love? (See 1 John 4:8.) Yes, but we also read in the same book, *"Therefore consider the goodness and severity of God: on those who fell, severity; but toward you, goodness"* (Romans 11:22). The word *"severity"* means "a cutting off." It checks with Jesus's teaching in John 15, that a branch in Him that did not bring forth good fruit was pruned—cut off (see John 15:6). God prunes us down to size when we get uppity and rebellious. This is a miracle.

There was a case of gross immorality in the Corinthian church. A young man was living in an incestuous relationship with his mother. The very concept of this cancer in the church makes a Christian shudder, or it should! The members of the church did not know what to do. They didn't like the situation and had, no doubt, often spoken, rather cautiously, to the two church members, but they refused to alter their filthy ways. Paul told these Christians they should have removed the offenders from the church, not allowed them to contaminate the whole body and even partake of communion! He told them what they must do: come together in the house of God, and in the name of Jesus Christ and by His power (miracle-working *dunamis* power). *"Deliver such a one **to Satan** for the destruction of the flesh, that his spirit may be saved in the day of the Lord Jesus"* (1 Corinthians 5:5). The whole church was commanded by God's servant to deliver him *over to Satan*, not to pray the prayer of deliverance from Satan, because the man and his mother were not repentant, and no one can be delivered who is in rebellion to God. They can only expect His miracle judgments.

What would happen to this young man? As the reference shows that it would be his flesh or body that would be judged, we must assume that he either became very sick in body or suffered some kind of accident. The purpose of this judgment would be to bring the young man up with a spiritual jerk and give him time to consider his evil ways, and so to cry out for his healing. Later, we know he was restored to the Corinthian church. (See 2 Corinthians 2:6.) He must have learned his lesson, and so did not lose his salvation. We often wonder why some people do get so sick! Sometimes, it might be that the Lord is dealing with them.

Some years ago, my wife and I had a very ugly situation of rebellion in the church, particularly against God's servant. It was not only hurting me and making it extremely hard to minister the Word to the flock, but it also carried the possibility of splitting the church, which is a very common thing today in some churches! My heart was almost breaking, for a true pastor still loves the rebellious sheep, and after everything had been tried in love, to no avail, my wife and I decided to give the rebellious ones over to Satan. The rebellious ones were smitten in their bodies and the whole unpleasant business was brought to an end. It makes me sad even to relate this happening, but the word of prayer from a servant of God, with others in the church, is mighty to the pulling down of strongholds. God's work—His church—must not be allowed to suffer and be prevented from manifesting the glory of God in our day and generation. *"For our God is a consuming fire"* (Hebrews 12:29).

How can we deal with those who try to infiltrate our churches with false doctrine?

> *And this occurred because of false brethren secretly brought in (who came in by stealth to spy out our liberty which we have in Christ Jesus, that they might bring us into bondage), to whom we did not yield submission even for an hour, that the truth of the gospel might continue with you.*   (Galatians 2:4–5)

Here is a most interesting account of true apostolic dealing with doctrinal error. Some people described as *"brethren,"* members of other assemblies possibly, came into their midst to try to bring them back into bondage of false teaching, possibly Judaic legalities of touch not, taste not, don't do it this way, etc. Did Paul give them a hearing? For, after all, philosophy tells us there are two sides to every question! Did he give them "equal time" as we are supposed to do in a democracy? Not so. He told them to get out and stay out within the hour, and used both his authority as an apostle and the power of the Holy Spirit. If they had stayed after such sharp admonition, no doubt they would have been in deep judgmental trouble. I can hear Paul saying, "Get out, in Jesus's name!" Was this a "Christian" act? Should we speak to brethren like that? Was it a Christian act for Jesus deliberately to whip the moneychangers in the temple area and cast them out with divine wrath? Some would think that Jesus was hardly a Christian at all, and certainly Paul must have been a monster.

When we think of the case of the two she-bears coming out of the wood to attack the fortytwo young men (probably teenagers) who insulted the prophet Elijah by jeering at him and calling him "old baldhead," we realize that the anger of God is swift against unseemly behavior toward His chosen servants. I know many reject this story as showing that God must be a monster and not a God of love, but it seems that wherever rebellion is found against God and the church, we find this wrong concept of God arising. The story, though terrible, agrees with the same principles that I have discussed in the New Testament. God is a God of judgmental miracles against those who mock Him. God is not mocked. He says so. Here the teenagers were injured in their bodies, the same as Elymas.

Was God wrong in opening the earth and swallowing up 250 men who offered incense to God when in a state of rebellion? (See Numbers 16:35.) Our offerings are repugnant to God if we do not obey Him. They are hypocritical. What about the case of thousands of Israelites being bitten by serpents because they rebelled? (See Numbers 21:6–7.) It seems that God's miracle-working judgments often become a blessing in disguise to arrest us in our rebellion. While lying on our backs, we have time to reflect a little and to read our Bibles afresh.

I am sure that as the church grows to maturity in our generation, we are going to see a great return of supernatural judgments, by miracles from God, to cleanse the church of rebellion and to cause fear to come upon the church, and to keep away those who would pervert the church. She is going to be a bride without spot or wrinkle or any such thing, and to get rid of a wrinkle, it becomes necessary to apply a hot iron with pressure.

14

THE CLAY AND THE WAX

*What shall we do to these men? For, indeed, that a notable miracle
has been done through them is evident to all who dwell in
Jerusalem, and we cannot deny it.*
—Acts 4:16

Reference to the above Scripture was made in chapter 1. The birthday
of the true church occurred in Acts, chapter 2. Let us never lose sight
of the fact that before Pentecost, Jesus Himself was the body of Christ,
and until He was crucified, He could not send the Holy Spirit to cohere
the initial 120 members into a corporate whole. Dr. William Smith, in
his *Bible Dictionary*, writes, "The day of Pentecost is the birthday of the
Christian church. Before Pentecost they had been individual followers
of Jesus; now they became His mystical body, animated by His Spirit."

Many have restricted the miracle of the rebirth to the total necessary
requirement for membership of the body of Christ, but we must bear in
mind that the teaching of Jesus to Nicodemus in John, chapter 3, was
given in the Old Testament dispensation, because the New Testament
did not come into effect until after the cross. It was just as possible to be

born again of the Spirit under the old covenant as under the new. The formation of the body of Christ on the Day of Pentecost was brought about by something more than the rebirth by the Spirit of God. It was the baptism of the Holy Spirit, another work of the Spirit, that created the true body of Christ, and this infilling was immediately accompanied by the miracle of speaking in tongues. The birth of the new body was evidenced by the birth cry from heaven. We emphasize this theological fact because we want to demonstrate that the true church began with a miracle and should continue with miracles. It is a miracle church. The conception of Jesus was a miracle; the resurrection was a miracle; and the subsequent outpouring of the Holy Spirit was a miracle. The forms of the old covenant gave place to the reality and substance of the new. It was a better covenant.

Following the exciting events of Acts 2 and Peter's initial sermon, a few days passed, and then God dropped His spiritual bomb into their midst. He caused a notable miracle to occur at the Gate Beautiful with the healing of the crippled man. This miracle caused such a stir that everyone in Jerusalem knew about it, without the aid of radio or television. God was working to a divine principle. Peter had preached the Word of God and God Himself had confirmed it. This is all according to the pattern of Matthew 10:7–8. Let us face the facts. The Word of God teaches that we should not only expect to preach or teach the Bible, but to have it confirmed by miracles. *"And they went out and preached everywhere, the Lord working with them and confirming the word through the accompanying signs* [miracles]" (Mark 16:20). Our problem in so-called Christian lands has been that the Word has been partly preached, often with mutilations, additions, and traditions, but it was never even expected that God in heaven would confirm the preaching with miracles, and so they did not happen.

With the healing of the crippled man, the church militant began its major offensive against sin and disease. God was determined to let Jerusalem know that His Son, whom they crucified, had indeed risen from the dead. How better to advertise the gospel! Every time someone prays and God answers from heaven, it is proof that Jesus lives and that He arose from the dead.

The rain falls on the just and the unjust (see Matthew 5:45), and the sun shines on the evil and the good. The Holy Spirit shines upon mankind like the sun, and some react like clay and become harder and harder. Other humans react like wax and become softer and softer. God can do nothing with baked clay, but He can mold the wax to His pattern. With the increase of the present outpouring of the Spirit upon all flesh (see Joel 2:28), the same miracles that bless some will be the cause of others becoming bitter, jealous, and more condemned. This is why Jesus spoke in parables, because He said His disciples would understand, but the religious leaders would be much more condemned if they heard Jesus speak in language they could understand. He knew their hearts.

> EVERY TIME SOMEONE PRAYS AND GOD
> ANSWERS FROM HEAVEN,
> IT IS PROOF THAT JESUS LIVES AND THAT HE
> AROSE FROM THE DEAD.

The healing of the crippled man brought blessing to thousands, but the reaction of the religious leaders was quite the opposite. They recognized that a notable miracle had occurred; they said they could not deny it. They were arrested by the Spirit into a place of impotent rage. They noted also that it was Peter and John who had worked the miracle. Peter said to the man, "*Such as I have give I thee*" (Acts 3:6). The crippled man received it by his faith, Peter gave it to him with his faith, and when the two came together a miracle took place. Yes, it is quite consistent that Peter and John worked the miracle, for Jesus had already commanded His disciples to heal the sick, because they had freely received from

Him and were expected to give freely. What had He given them? Paul called the ability *"gifts of healing...the working of miracles"* (1 Corinthians 12:9–10).

When the Holy Spirit came upon them in the upper room, the divine charismatic abilities were given with the Holy Spirit; they were integral in the Spirit. When they received the Holy Spirit from the risen Christ, they received His divine miracle-working attributes. These gifts (nine in number) are not given for personal use, or for personal blessing, but they are given to give, and to whom should we give them? Surely to the sick and crippled of our age. We transmit them after we receive them. We speak and He confirms our speech with a miracle; but if we never speak it, it will probably never happen.

Peter and John were all keyed up waiting for the great miracle to take place, and when they saw the crippled man they received a word of knowledge that this was the one God had chosen for the miracle. They ignored the plea for silver and gold and gave him healing, worth far more. Could it be that much of the church has been more interested in receiving silver and gold than in giving miracles?

Peter and John, who had been brought up beneath the spiritual headship of the priests, now found themselves under a greater Headship, that of Jesus, the chief High Priest. This High Priest rightly interpreted the Scriptures, thereby confounding the official custodians of the divine mysteries. The priests commanded them, with threats, that they should no more teach the Jews about these things. They were terrified that more miracles would occur; but Peter and John answered with divine anointing, *"Whether it is right in the sight of God to listen to you more than to God, you judge. For we cannot but speak the things which we have seen and heard"* (Acts 4:19–20).

The priests let them go, and they returned to the other new Jewish believers in Jerusalem, and they rejoiced together and had a prayer meeting. They reminded the Lord of the prophecies in Psalm 2 about kings and rulers rising up against the Lord and His Christ, and then they prayed, *"Now, Lord, look on their threats, and grant to Your servants that with all boldness they may speak Your word, by stretching out Your hand to heal, and that signs and wonders may be done through the name of Your holy Servant Jesus"* (Acts 4:29–30). They did not pray to play it safe; they were not cowed by the self-righteous priests; their one object was to preach and expect God to do His part by baring His arm in working many miracles in the immediate future. Their understanding of the preaching of the gospel of the kingdom was to expect miracles. If they had not occurred they would have been astonished. The place shook where they prayed, and they went out and demonstrated great power (*dunamis*—miracle power), thus proving the resurrection of Jesus. Here, it is stated that the working of miracles was the indisputable evidence of the resurrection. How many church buildings shake today!

It was at this point that great fear came upon the church: *"And through the hands of the apostles many signs and wonders were done among the people"* (Acts 5:12). Can we imagine the utter frustration of the religious leaders? More and more, miracles were proliferating throughout Jerusalem; the whole city was full of the news, and the very ones that the people had looked to as spiritual leaders turned out to have feet of clay, baked hard by the outpouring of the Spirit. Instead of the leaders with their theological degrees doing miracles, it was now seen that the men with feet of wax, whom they called "unlearned and ignorant men," were doing the "impossible." The religious leaders were shown up in all their fancy dress and spiritual impotence. Pride was too strong among most of them to humble themselves under the hands of these apostles and to receive forgiveness of sins and healings of mind and body, particularly from the spirit of jealousy.

Today, we are seeing the same thing, but as in those days many priests did believe, *"Then the word of God spread, and the number of the disciples multiplied greatly in Jerusalem, and a great many of the priests were obedient to the faith"* (Acts 6:7). In the old-line denominations, we are hearing of many priests and ministers who are being obedient to the faith and are receiving the baptism in the Spirit and entering into the life of the miraculous. The church is becoming one again, returning to preaching the Word, with the Lord confirming the Word with miracles.

Unfortunately, if history is our guide, many will also try to block the moving of the Spirit, for the charismatic move is challenging their formal methods of conducting religious services. This is most noticeable because of the large increase of charismatic books arising today, which is very disturbing to many of our evangelical brethren who have decreed the doctrine of dispensationalism. If they say it cannot happen today, then they have to pretend that it isn't happening all around them. Some ministers have been fired by their denominations or local church boards. The Spirit of God being breathed into their fading relevance has caused a hardening of the clay in their midst, even as in Stephen's day when he spoke out boldly and denounced these men, *"You stiff-necked and uncircumcised in heart and ears! You always resist the Holy Spirit"* (Acts 7:51). As they represented the state, they brought to bear their law of stoning, and the first martyr fell to the earth, the first of the martyr seeds that would bring forth a great harvest like unto Stephen. No one, apart from Jesus, spoke straighter to the religious leaders. Jesus said, *"Scribes and Pharisees, hypocrites!"* (Matthew 23:13). Would a Christian minister utter these words today?

We are glad that the late pope, the bishop of the Church of Rome, indicated his approval and blessing upon the present outpouring of the Holy Spirit upon Roman Catholics worldwide. This bodes well for a great renewal of the church within the Roman structure, but this, in turn, will bring enormous changes of practice and doctrine, which are already taking place now, in 1979. There is a real sense that Roman Catholics, in spite of their traditions, will receive the baptism in the Spirit with the sign of tongues more easily than many of the Protestants in their communions. The Catholics will be greatly encouraged by the presence of Cardinal Suenens of Belgium, who has received the Holy Spirit baptism, and he will no doubt act as a great strength to them. The editor of *New Covenant* magazine, Ralph Martin, whom I know, has written that there are three distinct rivers flowing today—one, the classic Pentecostal river made up of those denominations known as Pentecostal; the second, those who are receiving the baptism in the Spirit among the Protestants and Baptists; and third, the Roman

Catholic charismatics. These three rivers are flowing parallel at present, but they will shortly merge into one great, broad river, *"a river that I could not cross; for the water was too deep, water in which one must swim, a river that could not be crossed"* (Ezekiel 47:5). There will be an agreement on all essential doctrine in that day. While the three rivers are flowing separately, yet in the same direction, there is little point in raising acrimonious discussions on variant doctrinal issues. We are all aware of them, but God Himself will resolve the matter to everyone's complete satisfaction, for we shall see eye-to-eye in that day.

The Archbishop of Canterbury has also noted that there is an increase of interest in this renewed outpouring of the Spirit among Anglicans worldwide. It is recognized as a fact in many Anglican dioceses, including the one in Toronto, Canada. The outpouring of the Spirit is going to be received in our day, and multitudes of priests and ministers and their congregations will be baptized in the Holy Spirit and begin a renewed life in the Spirit, expecting and seeing miracles in their midst. Nothing can stop it today. *"This is the day the Lord has made; we will rejoice and be glad in it"* (Psalm 118:24).

15

HOW DO WE START?

God also bearing witness both with signs and wonders, with vari-
ous miracles, and gifts of the Holy Spirit.
—Hebrews 2:4

Many who are truly children of God by faith in Jesus Christ would frankly be at a loss to know how to anticipate miracles. It is clear from our study on the subject of miracles in the New Testament that these should always occur following the faithful preaching of the gospel of the kingdom; but after we have preached the full gospel, how are we to act or try to precipitate miracles? Is there anything we should do after preaching? We have been so used to preaching, and some have made it a regular practice to have an altar call, that our understanding of "what's next" seems to stop with our methodology.

Many have asked me, "How do we cast out a demon?" The idea behind the question is often fear that one day they might be faced with the necessity to do so. There is always a first time for every new experience, and assuming a demon is present, then Jesus tells us to cast it out in His name. We may not be sure, because we have not listened to the still, small voice of the Spirit giving us either the discerning of spirits or a word of knowledge; this may be beyond our spiritual understanding, but it is clear that where a demon is present, Jesus told us to cast it out! How do you cast an unwanted dog off your property? Do you pray and ask Jesus to do it for you, or do you take action by word and deed to evict the unwelcome stranger?

As I have recounted in my book *Dominion Over Demons*, there was a first time in my experience in 1948. 1 had tried praying for a man with congenital asthma by the only known methods of anointing with oil and *asking* Jesus to heal, but nothing happened! I did not know that I was doing it the wrong way. After prayer and some advice that was given to me, I decided I would deal with this man's sickness in an entirely different (yet scriptural) way. I addressed myself to the demon behind the sickness and said, "You foul spirit, come out of him in Jesus's name!" The demons of sickness immediately reacted and began to cough out of him accompanied by much mucous. I had precipitated a miracle, which may not have occurred unless I had rebuked the spirit behind the asthma. He was permanently healed.

While realizing the fact that spontaneous miracles do occur in right circumstances, it seems that we must do our part if we expect God to do His part. In many cases, Kathryn Kuhlman actually rebuked sicknesses in people when they came to the platform and she was face to face with them.

We have the story of the healing of Peter's wife's mother as a good guide to find out how Jesus healed her. There are three accounts in the gospel of this important healing, and all three give us a different aspect of truth, and I want to tie these together: in Luke 4:38–39, we find that Jesus *rebuked* the great fever; in Matthew 8:14–16, we read that Jesus *touched* her hand and the fever left her; and in Mark 1:30–31, we find that Jesus took her by the hand and the fever left her. Let us deal with the three things that Jesus did. He did *not* ask the Father to heal her for His sake. He took definite action, and I believe we should do exactly the same.

First, He rebuked the fever. The word *rebuke* means to set a weight upon; in other words, when Jesus opened His mouth and spoke to the spirit behind the fever, He put such an intolerable weight upon this demon spirit that it could no longer remain in such an uncomfortable situation. It left rapidly, to get away from the Spirit of God emanating from Jesus's presence and from His Word. It must be obvious that Jesus would not speak to an inanimate "something." He spoke to the spirit, which heard, understood, and obeyed. Only an intelligent being will do this.

THE TOUCH IMPARTS THE GIFT OF HEALING INTO THE SICK PERSON. LET US NOT FORGET THAT THE CHARISMATIC MANIFESTATION OF CHRIST CALLED *"GIFTS OF HEALINGS"* (1 CORINTHIANS 12:9), WHICH ARE WITHIN A HOLY SPIRIT-FILLED CHRISTIAN, GIVES ALL OF US THE ABILITY TO IMPART A PARTICULAR GIFT OF HEALING FROM THE MANY GIFTS OF HEALING WITHIN US.

Second, Jesus touched her with His hand. This is important, because He teaches us to lay hands on the sick so that they shall recover. The touch imparts the gift of healing into the sick person. Let us not forget that the charismatic manifestation of Christ called *"gifts of healings"* (1 Corinthians 12:9), which are within a Holy Spirit-filled Christian, gives all of us the ability to impart a particular gift of healing from the many gifts of healing within us. This charismatic ability has often been wrongly understood and interpreted to mean that the one who prays has "a gift of healing," rather like the healers of the occult groups. Some have a ministry of healing, and they are enabled to impart a particular healing for a particular sickness. It is the sick person who receives the gift! As we touch in faith, even a fingertip touch, the gift of healing flows into the sufferer to replace the sickness that has been rebuked. The sickness becomes paralyzed and bound. The touch imparts new health.

Third, Jesus took her by the hand and gently lifted her up, because He wanted to prove to her that to continue to lie in bed would be quite unnecessary, for she was healed! She might not have realized how wonderfully she was healed until she received practical help. Many times, when I prayed for people who have been paralyzed in an arm or leg, I have said, "Now move your arm." They shake their heads, for they know that in the past they could not do so! Their minds have not understood how a miracle takes place so silently. Then it becomes necessary to take their arms and begin to motivate them in Jesus's name. At first, this can produce some pain as the stiffness or soreness leaves, but the action of faith helps it to leave, and ease of movement begins to come. Sometimes, I have found it necessary to pray against the problem a second time, with the cooperation of the sufferer, and so often, the pain and stiffness give way to such prayer and action. As a person begins to act his own faith and walk, or run, or dance, the symptoms begin to go. Faith must be accompanied by action—as the lepers went, they were healed.

I remember praying for a woman named Mrs. Woods, in Toronto, some years ago. Her legs were swollen and painful with arthritis. She was sitting, so I took her hands and prayed, rebuking the sickness in Jesus's name. Then, I said, "Come on now, rise and be healed," so she acted on this instruction of faith and found that all the pain and stiffness had gone. She remained perfectly healed for years.

Jesus gives us this principle of faith in the story of the healing of the impotent man at the Pool of Bethesda. He had been lying down unable to walk for thirty-eight years—a long time—but Jesus said, *"Rise, take up your bed and walk"* (John 5:8). The man immediately arose, like Peter's mother-in-law, and took up his bed and walked. If he had not obeyed the words of Jesus, he would have remained in a procumbent position and not realized that after the command of faith he could walk. Our trouble today, especially in hospitals, is that we are called on to pray for people who have no intention of getting out of bed and walking, because they would not want to disobey their doctor's instructions! In fact, they would not expect to get out of bed and walk if a minister or a priest prayed for them. If the minister was so bold as to command them to get out of bed and start walking around the hospital ward, they would look upon him with horror and astonishment. It is this unbelief among Christians that is such a stumbling block to the working of miracles.

OUR TROUBLE TODAY, ESPECIALLY IN HOSPITALS, IS THAT WE ARE CALLED ON TO PRAY FOR PEOPLE WHO HAVE NO INTENTION OF GETTING OUT OF BED AND WALKING, BECAUSE THEY WOULD NOT WANT TO DISOBEY THEIR DOCTOR'S INSTRUCTIONS! IN FACT, THEY WOULD NOT EXPECT TO GET OUT OF BED AND WALK IF A MINISTER OR A PRIEST PRAYED FOR THEM.

A few years ago, I was called into a Scarborough, Ontario, hospital to pray for a Mr. Larry Snellgrove, an international director of the Full Gospel Businessmen's Fellowship. He had been rushed to a hospital with bleeding of the bladder, a serious thing indeed. Doctors found a growth in the bladder and planned to operate early the next morning. I prayed for him, rebuked the growth in Jesus's name, and, after a few words of encouragement, left the hospital. It was not long afterward, on the same evening, that Mr. Snellgrove telephoned to say he had signed himself out of the hospital, against the wish of the doctors, because he believed that he had indeed been healed at the time of the prayer of agreement. There was no visible evidence that healing had taken place, for he was still hemorrhaging, and this lasted for eleven days, days of testing. On the eleventh day, the bleeding stopped, and a few weeks later, he passed from his body granular matter. Some months later, he was examined by the doctors again, and they could find no trace of a tumor, for it had completely disappeared. Would this miracle have happened if he had not acted his faith, which in this case was basically, "Arise, take up your bed, and walk"? I may not know the answer, but it does seem that because he acted in accordance with Scripture he received a miracle.

It seems we must adopt this method if we are to expect to see miracles following our preaching. Let us remind ourselves of these three steps. (1) We address ourselves to the spirit behind the sickness and rebuke it. (2) We impart the necessary gift of healing by the laying on of hands. (3) We help the sick one to realize that by the stripes of Jesus they really are healed. In chapter 2, I told of the healing of the man with the locked spine. It was when he started to do what he had been unable to do for twenty years that he realized he had been healed, and he proved it by touching his toes. No doubt, he could have refused to believe, and so he would have stayed rigid.

I have seen cases of people in wheelchairs who have arisen and started to walk afresh. Often they will be weak, but as they continue to act their faith, the strength returns to them, given by Him who is the resurrection and the life. It is His life that quickens or brings strength back to our sick, tired bodies. It is real, but we must believe, and our belief will be shown by our actions. This is what James taught: "*What does it profit, my brethren, if someone says he has faith but does not have works? Can faith save* [or heal] *him?... Thus also faith by itself, if it does not have works* [or action], *is dead*" (James 2:14, 17). So many will say, in desperation, "I have all the faith in the world," and after prayer get no miracle. Faith alone will not heal you or show you your miracle; you must begin to act as though you have it.

When the mother of my eldest son's wife was healed of arthritis and bursitis, she was stiff with pain in shoulders and elbows. After rebuking the sickness, I took her arms and started slowly moving them. She felt great pain and her forehead broke out in sweat drops, but I ignored her cries and continued moving her arms. They got looser and looser, and the pain began to go. Then I took her knotted fingers and started to move them, and slowly, the pain and stiffness went out, and she has maintained her healing for some years. She goes around everywhere telling of her miracle. Without the healing power of the Lord, she would have been in a wheelchair by now.

Another daughter-in-law was able to turn hand spins after receiving prayer for a badly injured ankle. She had been given cortisone by her doctor because of the severe pain. Her mother had degeneration of the spine and had been told that she would shortly be confined to a wheelchair, but after prayer, she went back to the swimming pool and swam fifty lengths to prove her miracle. All these have held their healing miracle for years. In my own family alone, quite apart from the church of which I was proud to be the pastor, miracles have taken place as soon as faith action was taken.

I went to London, England, in 1974, and I met a woman who told me she was suffering so much from the bondage of arthritis, but she said, "I have never seen a miracle." Owing to the grip of the state church with its formal worship, it is not expected that worshippers will see miracles in their services, and this has bred, over hundreds of years, a dead unbelief for the supernatural. The whole emphasis is the worship that they give. They are not taught to expect anything in return. Sick people go to hospitals, not to churches for healing. They go to doctors, not to Jesus. They have faith in the efficacy of drugs, not of the blood of Jesus. They need encouragement and teaching. Preaching and praying for miracles in Europe is a very hard thing. They have never seen a miracle! I began to rebuke the spirit of arthritis in this lady, and slowly and stubbornly it began to respond, and finally began to cough out of her with deep coughing. After my return to Canada, this lady wrote telling of a definite improvement in her health. She was rejoicing.

The more faith that can be produced in the hearing of the gospel of the kingdom, the more quickly will the sicknesses leave the mind and body. This is why Jesus puts preaching first, to be followed by action on the part of the ministers and priests, who should then expect to see miracles taking place. They may happen slowly or quickly; this seems to depend on individual faith, and as we see healings taking place, our own faith grows stronger, so that we in turn may impart a miracle more easily to others. This prayer of faith that heals the sick is mutual. (See James 5:14–15.) This is why preaching must come first—because it inspires faith: *"So then faith comes by hearing, and hearing by the word of God"* (Romans 10:17). It may be true that our strong faith may bring a miracle to a person who has little or no faith, but without their own faith, they will be unable to maintain their healing, and they will probably get sick again.

THE MORE FAITH THAT CAN BE PRODUCED IN THE HEARING OF THE GOSPEL OF THE KINGDOM, THE MORE QUICKLY WILL THE SICKNESSES LEAVE THE MIND AND BODY. THIS IS WHY JESUS PUTS PREACHING FIRST, TO BE FOLLOWED BY ACTION ON THE PART OF THE MINISTERS AND PRIESTS, WHO SHOULD THEN EXPECT TO SEE MIRACLES TAKING PLACE.

On the last Sunday of 1974, a woman and her husband drove from Windsor, Ontario, just to see what our church was like. They had heard of us! They had no intention of asking for anything special. This woman had arthritis all over her body, but I preached on the receiving of miracles, and then some people went into the prayer room to receive theirs. A Presbyterian minister's wife had a leg lengthened by one inch—she had been wearing a built-up shoe. The woman from Windsor, who was originally from the Greek Orthodox Church, asked me to pray against her arthritis; so I asked her to sit down and examined the length of her legs. Sure enough, on the side of maximum pain (the left side) her leg was one inch shorter than the right. As I prayed, it came level with the other, and all pain instantly disappeared. The next day, she ran upstairs! The doctors had called it arthritis and treated it as such, without much results. Could it not have been caused by a pinched nerve in a crooked spine bringing arthritis pains throughout the nervous system?

Before returning home, she brought her husband and he also had a leg one-half-inch short, and it was made whole. He also had a touch of diabetes and we prayed for a miracle for this too—only time will show if he got this necessary miracle. More on this in the next chapter.

16

HOW TO KEEP YOUR MIRACLE

See, you have been made well. Sin no more,
lest a worse thing come upon you.
—John 5:14

Obviously, we are not made whole to live the old life that we used to live, for it was probably this way of life that brought our trouble upon us in the first place. No one repairs a house and leaves it without a tenant. Our bodies become the very temple of the Holy Spirit, and who ever heard of a temple that was run down and dilapidated and failing to bits in ruins? Satan knows that our bodies are dwelling places, for in the story of the unclean spirit that was cast out of a man, the spirit was determined to get back and hung around, waiting for a favorable opportunity, and said, "*I will return **to my house**"* (Matthew 12:44). It is a fact that our bodies do indeed become the dwelling place for God or the devil. It seems we just cannot occupy them alone and be neutral. We must have God or the devil to dwell with us. We get lonely otherwise!

It is very dangerous to be beautifully delivered by the power of Jesus and His blood, to have our house "swept and garnished" and then have no tenant inside except ourselves. Our body or house is first swept clean of all filth of the flesh (see 1 Peter 3:21) and then garnished with beautiful fittings; the walls become decorated with the luscious fruits of the Spirit; the furniture is heavenly and the carpets lovely. The gifts of the Spirit are available in every room and the glory of God covers the place like a cloud, so that everyone who enters will be blessed and healed also.

But there are some who feel they are healed because it is their inalienable right as a Christian and that it really does not matter too much how they live, because they believe "once saved, always saved," and that their names are in the Lamb's Book of Life. Whereas it is true that we do not inherit eternal life by our works, yet we do maintain our health by living close to God in this life; in fact, the very reason that we are delivered from the power of the enemy should cause us to live closer to the Lord than before we were set free. The love of God begets our love in return, and the definition of love is given by John the Beloved: *"For this is…love…that we keep His commandments"* (1 John 5:3). Love of God is not a sentimental, mushy kind of love, but a true obedience founded on deep reverential love.

According to the teaching of Jesus, it would be better not to have been delivered than that we should afterward live a loose backsliding life, for it is exactly at such a moment that the same evil spirit that was cast out will return into *his house* with seven other spirits worse than himself. Jesus said, *"And the last state of that man is worse than the first"* (Luke 11:26). This is a terrible prospect, and a solemn warning, that being a true, happy Christian is not a state that can be lightly handled. If you want a miracle in your life to deliver you from some oppressive satanic bondage of soul or body, you must be prepared to live all out for the Lord. In the Scripture, we have quoted at the beginning of this chapter, Jesus told us about the man who had an infirmity for thirty-eight years, who, to maintain his miracle, must *never sin again*. This is a tall order, isn't it?

There are several definitions of sin. Sin is transgression of the law (see 1 John 3:4), but John shows us that a true Spirit-filled, born-again Christian does not sin! *"All unrighteousness is sin, and there is sin not* *leading to death. We know that whoever is born of God **does not sin**; but he who has been born of God keeps himself, and the wicked one* [Satan] *does not touch him*" (1 John 5:17–18). There are two contrasting definitions of sin in the Bible: the sin of ignorance and the sin of presumption. (See Leviticus 4; Psalm 19:13.) The sin of ignorance is one we all commit, because we are still imperfect, but these are not sins that we willingly commit, because we love the Son of God. As soon as a sin that is caused by our imperfections becomes noticed as such, we immediately confess it, renounce it, and reckon it is under the blood of Jesus. The sin of presumption, however, is when we deliberately do something that is known by us to be contrary to God's will and Word. There is no forgiveness for such a sin until it is confessed and forsaken and put under the blood. The *"sin not leading to death"* is the sin of ignorance. A Christian who really loves the Lord has no desire to sin intentionally, and so, to use the simile given by John, "he keeps himself." This thought is taken from James, who wrote, *"To keep oneself unspotted from the world"* (James 1:27). The Christian who does this is described again by James in these words: *"But he who looks into the perfect law of liberty and continues in it, and is not a forgetful hearer but a **doer** of the work, this one will be blessed in what he does"* (verse 25).

So we should be able to see that the command of Jesus to sin no more, to avoid a worse condition of life (that is, by seven other spirits) is a most reasonable proposition.

AS SOON AS WE GET SICK, SATAN COMES
AGAINST US AT FULL FORCE AND TRIES BY
LYING AND BLUFF TO WIN US AWAY FROM THE
GLORIOUS PROMISES OF THE WORD OF GOD.

I have found in years of practical experience with the life in Christ that when, in God's overruling providence, He allows me to be attacked by Satan, whether in soul or body, it is a most humbling way of attracting my attention again to His promises of deliverance. *"Many are the afflictions of the righteous, but the* LORD *delivers him out of* **them all***"* (Psalm 34:19). As soon as we get sick, Satan comes against us at full force and tries by lying and bluff to win us away from the glorious promises of the Word of God. We are tested and refined, for God deals with us as sons and daughter, not as illegitimate heirs. (See Hebrews 12:8.)

Now, after experiencing deliverance of any kind, we are counseled in plain language to resist the devil for ourselves. The keeping of our house, the cleaning of the house, is our sole responsibility. We do not hire cleaning women to do these elementary chores—we do them ourselves, while others may encourage us to do a good job. Any pastor knows that it is not always easy to get some members to help in such chores as painting the church, cleaning out the washrooms, or caring for the garden, because many, unfortunately, think such work is too menial for them. In fact, I must express surprise that I have met some Christians like this. They would rather pay someone else to do it for them. This puts them in a position of superiority. The Bible teaches us that Jesus humbled Himself and became obedient. (See Philippians 2:8.) He was even born in a stable, by the will of God. Jesus started at the bottom. It seems to take some of us a little time to get there!

The greatest position of strength in the Lord is the position of true humility. Nothing is too much for us to do for God. We are so glad to have the opportunity to serve. I remember way back in 1940, in Dublin, Eire, I was first asked to administer the bread and wine in the Communion service to the people. My heart almost burst for joy at this great privilege. I, who had been a contaminated sinner, was now asked to serve the sacred elements of the body and blood of Jesus to the people. What an honor! I used to take every opportunity to serve at big healing conventions in the United States. I loved to take up the offerings, to do anything to help. Always be prepared to take the lowest station; otherwise how can He call you up higher?

Both Peter and James tell us the way to resist the devil. It is first from the position of true *humility*. "*Yes, all of you be submissive to one another, and be clothed with* **humility**, *for 'God resists the proud, but gives grace to the humble.'*... *The devil walks about like a roaring lion, seeking whom he may devour. Resist him, steadfast in the faith*" (1 Peter 5:5–6, 8–9). Note that our attitude at all times must be easily and willingly to be able to be subject to each other; as Paul puts it, "*in honor giving preference to one another*" (Romans 12:10), and thus, wear the very mantle of humility, not a false humility which is obvious to all, but the deep outworking of the love of Christ, loving and honoring the meanest among us. If this is our state, we can easily knock the devil out of the ring every time he enters in. James, in his fourth chapter, also tells us to humble ourselves and then resist the devil and he will flee.

Many, desiring to become humble, put on an act. They then pray, and say, "O Lord, keep me humble." This is not the prayer of faith, nor is it according to Scripture. Peter gave it to us straight. "*Humble yourselves under the mighty hand of God*" (1 Peter 5:6). We are the ones to take the humble position without God helping us. As soon as action is required, we are the first to volunteer, because there is no menial job that is beneath our dignity, because we have already taken the lowest place. We remember the words of our Savior, who told us to say, "*We are unprofitable servants. We have done what was our duty to do*" (Luke 17:10).

Humility is a most beautiful attribute of the Holy Spirit. By nature the Adamic man is proud, boastful, knowing nothing about God (see 1 Timothy 6:4), and we have to be most careful that these old traits of rebellion are put to death and buried in the waters of baptism. If pride rears its ugly head, we must immediately bring ourselves back into the place of humility before God, confessing it is all of Him and none of us. Let us not wait to be knocked off our horse as Paul was. (See Acts 9:4.) We should fall at His feet daily, and worship and adore Him, confessing that we know nothing apart from Him. Then our position is one of strength against the world, the flesh and the devil.

17

THE BRIDE PREPARES

*And the L*ORD *said to Moses, "...see that you do all those wonders before Pharaoh which I have put in your hand."*
—Exodus 4:21

The great story of the Exodus of Israel from Egypt is one of a succession of miracles whereby God bared His holy arm and delivered His people. They were not delivered by preaching, but by the supernatural.

Moses was a most unwilling candidate for the high office of being Israel's leader. He tried his best to argue his way out of a difficult situation. Why should he give up his church in the wilderness where he had sheep to supply his food and raiment? He had his tent-mansion and a wife and family. For forty years, he had lacked nothing and had grown into a rut. Many of us have, too. We resist changes in our religious thinking or our church orientation.

To a reluctant Moses, God gave two miraculous signs: one, the ability to deal with serpents; and the other, to cause healing to come to diseased flesh. (See Exodus 4.) After the initial shock of realizing that miracles could happen through Moses, God said that if the Israelites did not believe the first sign of handling serpents, they would believe the second sign of healing. However, the Lord warned that if anyone in Egypt refused both signs, then Moses was to continue to do miracles, which would be against Pharaoh, in order that by such pressure, he would let Israel go.

Moses took his rod in his hand (verse 20), which represented his God-given authority; today, it is represented by our Bible, God's final authority. It is with the Word of God today that we do miracles, so the masses may be convinced that God *is* God. When Moses used his rod, a miracle took place.

These miracles were: (1) God's rod turned into a serpent swallowing up all the little serpents produced by the magicians; (2) rivers turned to blood; (3) plague of frogs; (4) plague of lice; (5) plague of flies; (6) destruction of cattle; (7) plague of boils; (8) plague of hail; (9) plague of locusts; and (10) plague of darkness. It was only when the blood was applied that the miraculous deliverance of the first-born of every family and their cattle was accomplished. This represented the church of the first-born, and today, we must be born from above to be members of this New Testament church. (See Hebrews 12:23.)

It was the shedding of the blood of Christ that delivered us out of spiritual Egypt (see Revelation 11:8), and we are living in the days of the second Exodus, as spiritual Israel is being brought out of captivity from the world system known as Babylon or confusion, into the law and order of God's kingdom on earth.

The Lord does not have to invent new ideas to do the same job. If miracles delivered ancient Israel out of bondage into freedom, so likewise, exactly the same methods will produce the same results in our generation. In the interim period between the old covenant and the new, Jesus came to deliver Israel again with miracles. The first was the casting out of demons from the man in the synagogue in Capernaum; the second, the healing of Peter's mother-in-law. (See Mark 1:23–31.) Notice the same order—first handling serpents, and second dealing with disease. Jesus then handed this ability to His twelve apostles by giving them

His power (*dunamis*, miracle) and authority to cast out demons and to heal diseases. (See Luke 9:1–2.) His purpose was to educate His men, the very foundations of the coming New Testament church, to deliver Israel as Moses had done. When this proved successful with the twelve, He multiplied this ability by giving the same power and authority to seventy additional men, who went out into all the towns and villages round about and made the gospel work! These men were astonished and exclaimed, "*Even the demons are subject to us in Your name*" (Luke 10:17). They cast out demons and healed the sick after saying, "*The kingdom of God has come upon you*" (Matthew 12:28). What a simple sermon! Anyone can say that and then go ahead and prove it! Sermons without miracles may appeal to the intellect, but they will never help in casting out demons and healing sicknesses.

THE LORD DOES NOT HAVE TO INVENT NEW IDEAS TO DO THE SAME JOB. IF MIRACLES DELIVERED ANCIENT ISRAEL OUT OF BONDAGE INTO FREEDOM, SO LIKEWISE, EXACTLY THE SAME METHODS WILL PRODUCE THE SAME RESULTS IN OUR GENERATION.

It may be a bold statement to make, and I believe it is entirely prophetic in content, but the day is fast coming upon the church when she will only use those methods to deliver herself. Already today, in 1979, I am personally seeing men and women delivered, healed, and filled with the Spirit every week in our home church in Canada, quite apart from those similarly blessed in the various cities and countries that I am privileged to visit. The pattern is always the same, first to open the Bible and show people what is meant by the kingdom of God being among them, and then to pray for them and *expect* miracles to happen, and *expect* demons to come out of many crying with loud voice!

In Revelation 19:7, the cry goes up among the righteous and angels in heaven, "*The marriage of the Lamb has come, and His wife has made herself read.*" How is the wife of Jesus to make herself ready? How does any bride make herself ready for a wedding? By working at it. Every detail must be right. The marriage garment must be without spot or wrinkle. The body must be washed and clean. Suitable perfume must be applied. Her hair must be perfectly styled. Her flowers must all express joy and beauty. It takes a lot to prepare a bride. It costs money, too! Let us take a look at the bride of Jesus today. James asks the valid question, "*Is anyone among you sick?*" Surely the answer must come back, "Oh yes, I am sick in my mind and body, and there is to be a wedding. What shall I do to prepare myself?" James tells us, "*Call for the elders of the church*" (James 5:14). What for? Why not call for the medical men and the psychiatrists? Are not these the ones to prepare the bride? No, the elders. Why? Because they will pray the prayer of faith, and the bridegroom Jesus in heaven will send all the miracle-working power of His Holy Spirit into the sick people and heal them and cast all the demons out of them when the elders of the church use His name and authority and exercise it. They must make the gospel work!

It seems also that the bride will carry a lamp, with a bright-burning flame, because the lamp is full of pure oil, representing the Holy Spirit. It does seem, if we can understand anything from the parable of the wise and foolish virgins of Matthew 25, that those who had lamps but no oil were not ready! How wonderful has been the teaching about the baptism of the Holy Spirit in our generation, but there are some who still resist. God gives a whole generation for the bride to prepare herself for a marriage of eternity.

As we look at the various fragmented denominations of the whole church today, we surely must cry out in alarm. She is *not* ready by a country mile! Oh yes, there are many, many signs that she is doing something about it. The whole charismatic move of God is supplying the elders to help in the preparation. The members of the bride are being convicted, and they are coming for healing and for deliverance. They are receiving the baptism in the Spirit; they are exercising the gifts of the Spirit; they are healing each other in Jesus's name.

Don't get hung up on only using elders. There are not enough of them to do it alone. We need every laborer in the wheat field—men and women and young people, but all working under the help and discipline of the eldership. God doesn't set apostles, prophets, evangelists, pastors, and teachers just to embarrass the established denominations, but to deliver their members into the glorious liberty of the gospel. Out of darkness into light, out of bondage into freedom. No wonder Paul called it *"glorious liberty of the children of God"* (Romans 8:21), and he used the Greek word *teknon*, which means "baby children," ones who have not matured. This is what is happening. God is pouring out His Holy Spirit all over the world onto babes in Christ emerging from the shadows of their denominations.

Many classic Pentecostals find it hard to believe that Roman Catholics could even be children of God, but the Lord began to baptize them in the Spirit and they began to speak in tongues, so some said that these were phony baptisms. Their idea seems to have been that God could not give His Spirit to someone who held doctrinal error. But don't Protestants hold doctrinal error also? Is God going to wait until every member of His bride believes doctrine identically the same as all other members? Not so. The baptism of the Spirit is being given in answer to personal faith and the present need to prepare the bride for the marriage.

Without the oil, there would be no healing or deliverance from binding demon powers. Jesus set the pattern in Matthew 8:16 by casting out spirits *and* healing everybody. This same pattern is going to be performed in our generation by us.

It has pained so many to realize that sick people in churches may be afflicted by evil spirits called "spirits of infirmity" or weakness. The clergy have not been prepared for such a revelation. For one thing, they were never taught anything about it in seminary, and for another thing, it never happened in their denomination; but it is happening today for all to see or read about. Is God going to be circumscribed by the limitations of our theological seminaries or Bible schools? Must He only do it our way and not His way? You remember that Amos wrote, *"Can two walk together, unless they are agreed?"* (Amos 3:3). We may be quite sure that Jesus is not going to agree with us! It is we who are going to agree with Him! If we are to walk with Him eternally it will be on His terms and doctrine, not on ours! We may delude ourselves and say that our doctrine is the same as His, but suppose it isn't. We are then in a mess. It should be our delight to know God's ways. We should spend this whole generation seeking God's ways, and in order to do this we shall have to listen to the Holy Spirit after we have received Him in our personal Pentecost. Did not John clearly tell us, *"But the anointing which you have received from Him abides **in you**, and you do not need that anyone teach you"* (1 John 2:27)?

IT SHOULD BE OUR DELIGHT TO KNOW GOD'S WAYS. WE SHOULD SPEND THIS WHOLE GENERATION SEEKING GOD'S WAYS, AND IN ORDER TO DO THIS WE SHALL HAVE TO LISTEN TO THE HOLY SPIRIT AFTER WE HAVE RECEIVED HIM IN OUR PERSONAL PENTECOST.

After a Roman Catholic or a Protestant or a Baptist receives Acts 2:4 and speaks in tongues, they are then in a position to be taught of the indwelling Spirit, who will teach them and guide them into all truth. (See John 16:13.) The truth that the indwelling Spirit will teach us will agree with men qualified by the Spirit to teach in the church, known as teachers, one of the five ministry gifts of New Testament eldership. Our human spirits will witness to the Holy Spirit working in many different ways in a fully charismatic fellowship, and we shall all recognize the truth, and error will melt away. It will take the bright light from our burning lamps to do it. If our lamps have gone out, we shall only be led by men with their theological darkness, and this will never prepare the bride for the coming of the bridegroom!

Let us be warned not to go off into spiritual corners and ignore the men of God that He is raising up in this day and say we do not need them. We need each other, and every new facet of discovered truth will be shared with the whole body by the Spirit and by each other. We will share with each other rather than teach each other.

The two signs that Moses used will be the two signs that we shall use—miracles and healings, plus a whole catalog of New Testament signs and wonders and miracles of a greater dimension than in the early church. Every day, today, is an exciting day—it can be for you. Why not start now preparing yourself for His coming, so that you also can be without spot or wrinkle, so that you can have your miracle, your healing and your baptism in the Spirit? What is stopping you? Man or denomination? Husband or wife? Pride?

John saw the bride prepared. *"One of the seven angels...talked with me, saying, 'Come, I will show you the bride, the Lamb's wife'"* (Revelation 21:9). Inevitably, the time is approaching for the coming of Jesus for a perfected church. Will you be one of the wise or foolish members of the church? Will you be ready? John speaks of those who will be ashamed of themselves at His coming. (See 1 John 2:28.) Some have suggested that the Greek word here is very strong and means they will appear to be paralyzed. They will realize they have not made themselves ready. They did not believe all this teaching about healing, demons, and the baptism in the Spirit. Their churches taught that these signs were not for today. During the war in England, no one ever saw a banana, but it would have been foolish to say they were not for today, because they had a glut of them in Jamaica! There was a time when they were "not for to-day"—between 1940 and 1945 in Europe, but afterward, bananas came back again. So today, the gifts of the Spirit are available and there is a glut of them. All we have to say is "Come and feed at the Master's table. There is plenty for all."

God help us to be ready on the day He comes for His church. Help me to make myself ready while I have time. Amen.

CONCLUSION

If they do not hear Moses and the prophets, neither will they be persuaded though one rise from the dead.
—Luke 16:31

In the present charismatic renewal of the whole church, God is forcing Himself upon an unbelieving people by signs and miracles. These will increase rapidly. There will be mass healings and miracles taking place in huge outdoor meetings that cannot be denied. However, although they cannot be denied, many will not believe, because they do not wish to believe. Believing would alter their lifestyles!

The religious council, led by the high priest Annas, challenged the apostles, saying, *"By what power or by what name have you done this?"* (Acts 4:7). They could not deny the miracle of the healing of the lame man, for they admitted, *"For, indeed, that a notable miracle has been done through them is evident to all...and we cannot deny it"* (Acts 4:16)! This healing was admitted to be notable, and it was intended to be, for this means that God intended the whole of Jerusalem to take note that His Son, Jesus, had indeed risen from the dead and was alive and doing miracles. There is no evidence that Annas or Caiaphas ever accepted the person of Jesus as Savior, but they were given every opportunity to do so. They were without excuse. We believe that this is God's pattern and purpose today, to make it obvious to the whole church that He desires to heal and restore every sick Christian.

From Australia comes an amazing story. It was told by Pastor Leo Harris of Adelaide in his magazine, *Impact*. In 1975, three Christian businessmen heard that students in a certain public school were allowed to play with Ouija boards. They were so alarmed that they visited the principal, who ridiculed their protests, saying he did not understand how it worked, but he admitted it did work and it gave the students lots of fun. The three Christian men then walked through the school and discovered where the children played with these boards. They entered the room and again tried in vain to teach them the extreme danger of contacting demon spirits through Ouija boards. The children just laughed at them, and suddenly the wrath of God came upon one of these good men and looking at the board he said, "I rebuke the spirit in that Ouija board in Jesus's name!" Immediately, the board disintegrated into many parts. The resident demon had been expelled from inanimate matter. I told this story to a charismatic minister of an historic church and he said he would not dare to tell it to anyone in his church or denomination! Why not?

This story reminds us of the one in which a woman in Medellin, Colombia, threw her holy medal into the fire when she accepted Jesus as Savior, and, at the same instant of time, another holy medal in a box in her home at a distance exploded, and when she opened the box on returning home, there was a pile of dust. Again, a resident demon was cast out violently from inanimate matter. Many just laugh when we warn them that an idol brought from a foreign land may well have an evil spirit living right in their home to visit sickness and trouble upon them. We are awakening today to a greater awareness of the reality of our supernatural God and His Son, Jesus.

I believe that when the emblems of the communion service are prayed over by the minister, they are, in effect, impregnated by the Holy

Spirit. The Roman Catholics go a little further and teach that the bread has actually mysteriously changed its state and represents the "real presence of Jesus." The realization that personal evil can dwell in inanimate wood or stone must teach us that the Spirit of God can dwell in consecrated communion bread.

I realize that many will refuse to believe such things, but we need to keep well in mind that Jesus said we would do His works, but we would do *greater* works in our day. (See John 14:12.) Our mind boggles at such a thought that we in our day would do greater works than Jesus. It is hard enough to try to teach people that we can and should do the works that Jesus did, if we exercise enough faith, but to expect miracles of a dimension not compassed by the canon of the Scripture is to invite unbelief and ridicule.

A woman and her husband flew from California to Toronto to see me. Her story was strange. From time to time, she was attacked by demons that stiffened her body, and then an icy feeling came over her and her blood ran cold. She was quite powerless under these attacks, and then, suddenly, strange scratch marks would appear on her arms, about four to six inches in length, although the skin was not broken. She showed these marks to my wife and me. We prayed for her by rebuking these spirits in Jesus's name, and she began to sob uncontrollably for about one hour as they were progressively cast from her. Her husband looked on in astonishment! How can evil spirits attack a woman and leave visible marks on her body? She was a professing Christian and associated with the charismatic movement in her hometown. It would have been cruel to say, "She could not possibly have a demon," and just shrug off all responsibility as many would do. God is forcing us to realize that things are happening today for which we have no previous theological understanding, and therefore, no expertise to deal with the unknown. We are on the verge of the greatest breakthrough of the Spirit of God in the history of the world.

Another case that happened in our experience about the same time concerned a woman who came to us when we were visiting Dallas, Texas. She asked for prayer because she had breast cancer that had gone into her lymph glands. In the natural, there was little hope apart from a strange, unexpected remission. My wife and I explained to her that this was probably caused by an evil spirit of infirmity that was trying to destroy her life. She was a Christian, working among young people. As we began to take our authority over these malign forces, she began to cough deeply and mucous began choking out of her. I tell these things to show that we should not be afraid or appalled. God is trying to get our attention! Suddenly, we heard, "*Nein, nein, nein.*" We listened again, and this time the strange voice said, "*Nein, nein, ich komme nicht!*" The demon in a southern Texas woman was speaking to us in pure German, refusing to come out. How can we explain these happenings? How can a demon speak German? Quite easily, for it had previously lived in a German-speaking person and was probably liberated at his death, when it would attempt to find another body to inhabit and bring death upon its next victim. Many find it hard to believe in the sign miracle of speaking in other tongues, but when we show that demons also can speak other languages, one can see fear coming on their faces. When the Holy Spirit inhabits the human body, He can give many languages to the Spirit-filled Christian in whom He dwells. Satan also counterfeits all the gifts of the Holy Spirit.

It is written of the antichrist that he, energized by Satan, "*performs great signs*" (Revelation 13:13). We should remember that the meaning of the word *antichristos* is "one who comes in the place of Christ"—an imitator of Christ, claiming His authority and ability. By demonic powers, he imitates the power of Christ. We have many antichrists operating in the religious field today. They are active in the midst of the church.

One of the most challenging Scriptures in the Bible is found in Matthew 21:22: "*And **whatever things** you ask in prayer, **believing**, you will receive.*" On another occasion, two blind men came to Jesus, and He asked them, "*Do you **believe** that I am able to do this?*" They said to Him, "*Yes, Lord.*" Then He touched their eyes, saying, '*According to your faith let it be to you.*' And their eyes were opened" (Matthew 9:28–30). Here, we see the simplicity of coming to Him *in faith*. Nothing can be refused if we come in faith, and it seems that whatever our problem, mental or physical, it will constitute a miracle when we experience deliverance from it. Jesus is waiting anxiously for us to stretch out the hands of faith and receive our miracle.

The problem all began in the garden of Eden, when Adam and Eve partook of the fruit of the *knowledge* of good and evil. They did not have this intellectual ability in the garden because they lived solely by faith in God and His Word. The glory of God covered them and they had unbroken fellowship with the Father. It was only when they started to try to use their own wisdom, which, of course, did not agree with God's revealed wisdom, that they got into very severe trouble and could no longer walk with God in that pure, innocent way.

As we educate our children today, they begin to think they know more than God, and so, they never expect a miracle, even if they go to some cold, formal, intellectual church every Sunday. Anyone who dares to believe that God works miracles today would be considered a fool, but when they see a miracle, they will ascribe it to the power of the mind. One moment, we change from a fool to one who has super power of the mind able to work "mind miracles." They will not admit that the miracle, which they cannot explain by intellectual means, must be of God if the prayer is made in the name of Jesus. *"By what power or by what name?"* (Acts 4:7), asked the scribes. It is the power of God revealed in answer to the prayer in the name of Jesus. *"There is no other name under heaven given among men by which we must be saved"* (verse 12). Once again, the word for *"saved"* is *sozo,* which means "saved, healed, made whole, delivered, and set free"!

Once man is put in the position of having to admit a miracle, he has to make a quick decision about his ideas of God, and human pride is a very strong factor that keeps multitudes chained in ignorance, which they call wisdom. The knowledge of good and evil is too much for mankind. Satan told Eve that when she ate of the fruit of the tree, she would *"be like God"* (Genesis 3:5), and man loves to think of himself as a little god or deity, knowing so much more than his fellows and certainly much more than God Himself.

The evangelical church has basically rejected the miracle of tongues, and many of the classic Pentecostal churches have used the same excuses to reject the ministry of casting out demons; the next wave that is now coming in is of mass miracles, and the charismatic movement must be careful not to make the mistake of rejecting miracles as the norm.

I was talking to a Roman Catholic brother from Ottawa recently, and I asked him how many in his congregation had spoken in tongues. He replied, "Twenty-two! *But* soon they will all have the baptism in the Spirit!" This is expectant faith, and will be rewarded by the whole congregation receiving the sign gift miracle of tongues. Following close after this experience in local churches, we must expect everyone to believe God for a miracle of healing or restoration, and in this way, all sick people in our congregations will be made whole (*sozo*). It has come as a great shock to many pastors when some of their people have been prayed for and immediately demons have manifested themselves and come out to the astonishment of all. This is how God means it to be, for we truly believe God is pressing hard for a decision today, first among His children and then among the world.

There came a time of decision in Joshua's life when he challenged Israel to *"choose for yourselves this day whom you will serve"* (Joshua 24:15). This challenge is again being forced upon us because of world events. God is intervening in the affairs of men, for He has come down to deliver us out of the hands of our enemies. (See Luke 1:71.) The deliverance of Israel under the old covenant was wrought by miracles by the hand of God alone. There is a Second Exodus taking place today, and God's New Testament Israel people in our churches are again being delivered by miracles. The final miracles will take place when, once again, the whole Christian church understands the power that is in the blood of Jesus and uses it by sprinkling it on their hearts and homes, and God will see the blood and the great final Passover will take place. The firstborn ones who have been born again of the Spirit will be healed and delivered. The miracle of Holy Spirit fire is now being seen in our churches, bringing healing and life back into our lives instead of empty form and ceremony. (See Exodus 9:23.) The frogs of the false demons are being seen in our land (see Revelation 16:13; Exodus 8:6), and the darkness that can be felt is evident in every major city of the world— gross darkness of satanic delusion and unbelief (see Exodus 10:22; Isaiah 60:2). Instead of the brook Kidron, being dyed red with the blood of the temple sacrifice, typical of the blood of Jesus, we have had rivers of blood, shed in the world wars. (See Exodus 7:21.) The plagues are upon us, but New Testament Israel, the church of the firstborn (see Hebrews 12:23), will be delivered because Jesus made an atonement for us. His shed blood will bring us salvation and healing.

It would seem to me that the more daring the faith of the minister, the more probability of a miracle taking place. I must emphasize the great need for daring faith in commanding a miracle to take place. Sicknesses must be commanded to leave; physical deformities must be commanded to go and bodies to be made whole. Where the nature of a human has been gravely distorted by an incursion of demons, then the evil spirits must be commanded to leave the personality of the sufferer.

A man came to see me from Alberta recently. He had been mixed up in the occult and he was extremely depressed to the point of having little interest in life at all. This dangerous state will often lead to chronic depression and schizophrenia. The demons causing the trouble were firmly commanded to leave in Jesus's name. They did not move immediately, so we suggested that the man start pleading the blood of Jesus to help his deliverance. Within a short time, he suddenly started to speak in tongues as the Holy Spirit came in, and then the deliverance started. The demons were ejected by choking through his throat and continued for about fifteen minutes. The result was amazing. His whole countenance changed from torment to joy, and while he was with us for a few days, his face was beaming. Jesus delivered him by a miracle.

A woman came into church hobbling on an aluminum hand crutch with four feet. She walked with great difficulty and was assisted by her two daughters. She was driven in from Niagara Falls, Ontario. We ministered to her. The Lord straightened her back, realigned her hips, and adjusted her shoulders. She walked perfectly, without the hand crutch, and they all wept for joy. Later, she left the church and gave us the crutch for a souvenir. I dared to ask her age. She said she was eighty-three, and she walked *perfectly*.

There is no end to this ministry. It is just beginning. We are learning to *enforce* miracles in the name of Jesus. It seems the more we command them, the more they happen. As faith rises in the church, and especially among the ministers of the church, so will miracles increase. We again remind ourselves that Jesus could do no miracles in His hometown of Nazareth (because of their unbelief).

Many are afraid that if they pray, command, and do their best, nothing will happen! I would suggest that if this is our approach, nothing will ever happen! The more we exercise faith, the more faith we generate, both in ourselves and in those for whom we pray. We must dare to try, and we shall be increasingly satisfied with the results that we shall see. We shall get bolder and bolder in our faith, and miracles will increase in number.

The manifestations of all the gifts of the Spirit (see 1 Corinthians 12:8–10) are miraculous. These gifts should be the normal in our churches today, and the more they operate, the more faith will be generated, and the greater the miracles that will take place. This is an exciting age in which we live. We must attempt great things and expect great things, and they will happen. This is the way of faith.

With God, all things are possible to them that believe.

THE PROPHETIC WORD

CONTENTS

FOREWORD

It has been my privilege to have read this book before publication. My strong impression is that it will become a valuable addition to the available literature on the subject with which it deals—the last day outpouring of the Spirit and the manifestation of the gifts, or *charismata*.

The author possesses certain unique advantages in preparing a volume of this nature. Some ministers have exceptional talent to put their knowledge into print. On the other hand, there are gifted writers who have attempted to deal with this subject, but who have had little practical experience in the manifestation of the gifts. In the case of Rev. Whyte, however, he not only has had the benefit of long experience as a pastor, in which he has had an unusual ministry in the operation of the gifts, but he is also articulate with the pen and able to express himself in clear and lucid language. It is one thing to manifest a gift of the Spirit, and it is another thing to thoroughly understand the special problems involved in the local church where such gifts are operative.

In perusing the manuscript, I have noted that Rev. Whyte has given some excellent instructions on the working of the revelation gifts. There is, unfortunately, much misunderstanding and misinformation on this subject. The writer has given us some wise and illuminating counsel concerning the operation of this important group of related gifts.

There is a special reason why I believe that the appearance of this book is timely. As most people know, there has of late been a remarkable acceptance of the charismatic gifts in the historic denominations—a fact that has been widely publicized in national periodicals. Thousands of people, who, in years past, have thought of Pentecost as something beneath their dignity to consider, have suddenly discovered that these manifestations of the Spirit are altogether real and genuine, and meant for them. For indeed, Pentecost is not the monopoly of any group, but it is a blessing that God has promised would be poured out on all flesh.

We are certain that this book will find a wide field of usefulness throughout the whole church of Jesus Christ.

—*Gordon Lindsay*
August 1964

1

I WILL POUR OUT MY SPIRIT

It has been said that if the apostle Paul came to one of our modem cities, he would be most perplexed if he entered into some of our churches. The mode of worship, the forms and ceremonies, the robes, the unabashed entertainment, and the absence of the gifts of the Spirit would cause him astonishment, and if he was ever invited to preach in these churches (which is most improbable), he would preach such truths as would shock the worshippers, and it is doubtful if many would shake his hand as he left the church—not having received a love offering!

Christian magazines have carried articles on the present outpouring of the Spirit in the historic churches, which have apparently upset some who have been taught "dispensational truths"—that charismatic gifts were only for the early church, but certainly not for the sophisticated church of today. A certain pastor of a dispensational church wrote a letter to one magazine stating that these reports of a renewed outpouring of tongues, interpretation, and prophecy could not possibly be true, because they were not for today, and even if they were, God would not give these gifts to Episcopalians, for of all Christian communions, they are the most carnal! What a Christ-like spirit indeed!

In spite of man's monumental unbelief, God is, nevertheless, pouring out again His Spirit upon all flesh, in exactly the same manner as He did in the early church, with the same purpose in mind—that we may all be one *in spirit*. There is no denominational favoritism, no hit-and-miss watering—for this revival is coming down on all flesh. Roman Catholics are being filled with the Spirit, even Jews are being converted to Christ and filled with the Spirit, and in each case, the manifestation is the same—*glossolalia*, or "other tongues."

We repeat, the manifestation is invariably the same, each one filled overflows like a fountain, and out of his or her mouth comes the Word of God in the form of *glossolalia*. This single fact has produced the continual question: "Why tongues?" The purpose of this book is to answer that question, and to show the purpose of God in this final outpouring of the Spirit upon all flesh, with the accompanying signs and gifts of the Spirit.

It was Joel who prophesied this outpouring. The emphasis was that our sons and daughters would prophesy, which was again reemphasized in the account in Acts chapter two where we are told that "my servants" and "my handmaidens" would prophesy. (See Acts 2:16–18, 28–32.) From this, we conclude that it is God's unchanging purpose in this dispensation and generation that "His servants," i.e., His ministering servants, pastors, elders, deacons, etc., should "prophesy" and that the women, i.e., pastor's wives, deaconesses, Sunday school teachers, etc., should also prophesy. As our sons and daughters are also included, we understand also that it is God's will for our children growing up in our churches to be so affected by this last day outpouring of the Spirit that they also shall prophesy! This surely adds up to the fact that all our churches should be composed of members most of whom should prophesy. What tremendous churches—churches in which the apostle Paul would feel quite at home, and in which his ministry would be received with gladness and praise to God. He would be free to teach on 1 Corinthians 12, 13, and 14, without embarrassment!

On the day of Pentecost, the birthday of the Christian church, this prophecy received its initial fulfillment. This fulfillment was only partial, and we believe it receives its fullest consummation in our day. When the Holy Spirit was outpoured on the 120, without exception, they commenced to speak in other languages, sixteen of which were understood by Jews coming from surrounding nations in which they had been born, and which languages they spoke in addition to Hebrew and Aramaic. Out from the mouths of 120 disciples came the Word of God—the *Logos*—in unknown tongues. This was the pattern, and this pattern is being faithfully reproduced in our day all over the world.

Peter quoted freely from Joel to show that this supernatural demonstration was *a fulfillment* of prophesying. It has been common theology to teach that prophesying carries the restricted meaning of "preaching," and whereas we believe that Holy Spirit-anointed preaching should always be inspired utterance, yet we also believe the words "to prophesy" carry a far deeper connotation.

THE INITIAL EVIDENCE OF TONGUES IS THE
BEGINNING OF A SUPERNATURAL OUTFLOW
OF THE WORD OF GOD BY HIS SPIRIT THAT
WILL FINALLY PUT SATAN OUT OF BUSINESS.

The initial evidence of speaking in tongues at Pentecost was put under the heading "prophecy," for it was God forthtelling through his 120 disciples, and they heard *them speaking in our own tongues the wonderful works of God* (Acts 2:11). This was a manifestation of pure prophecy. We wish to try and demonstrate that *glossolalia* is one of the forms of prophecy referred to by Joel, and that without this initial prophetical utterance, it is doubtful that the other forms of inspired utterance can be brought forth. The initial evidence of tongues is the beginning of a supernatural outflow of the Word of God by His Spirit that will finally put Satan out of business. It is the Sword of the Spirit, which is the Word of God, unleashed from heaven against Satan's kingdom on earth.

There is much more in "tongues" than meets the eye—or the ear! *"If anyone speaks, let him speak as the oracles of God"* (1 Peter 4:11). Broadly speaking, "prophecy" is the speaking forth of the Word of God—under the inspiration of the Holy Spirit. When Jesus was here on earth in His own personal body—the body of Christ—it was said of Him, *"No man ever spoke like this Man!"* (John 7:46). He Himself said that "of Himself He could do nothing." (See John 5:19.) The words He spoke were not His words, but were received from His Father. Every word spoken by Jesus came directly from heaven; He did nothing, He said nothing, He thought nothing, apart from what He received from His Father. He had no original philosophical thought, He had no personal opinion, He did what He saw the Father do and spoke what He heard the Father speak. He was the verbal expression of the Father—the *Logos* of God.

In Hebrews 11:3, we read that *"by faith we understand that the worlds were framed by the word of God, so that the things which are seen were not made of things which are visible."* God did not create something out of nothing, as some have taught, He created matter out of "things which do not appear," in other words, matter is a physical expression of spiritual forces already in existence and which belong alone to God, who is *Life* and *Creation* Himself. It was the speaking *Logos* that created substance out of spiritual forces. How near is the physical realm to the spiritual! This same creative word that was in Jesus now comes into all the members of the body of Christ when they receive the baptism in the Spirit and speak in other tongues.

In the beginning, at creation, the Father spoke, the Word proceeded and the Holy Spirit moved upon His creation. God *said*…and it was so. He created light, firmament, waters, grass, herbs, stars, fish, animals, birds, and finally, the Trinity created man, the highest created being of God, His masterpiece, after His own image. Can we not see that if God created matter from His own spiritual but invisible forces, and then breathed His own life into bodies composed of matter, then when Satan invades such delicate creations, it is necessary to speak the Word in faith, and we in Christ are able to reverse the processes of destruction, because the words we speak are Spirit and life to those who receive? The evil spiritual invasion by Satan and his emissaries is forced to give way before the power and authority of the *Logos* which created matter!

The centurion understood this principle. His servant was lying shaking with palsy, and the centurion said that it was necessary to *"only speak a word, and my servant will be healed"* (Matthew 8:8). When Jesus spoke and said, "Be healed," it was so, and his servant was healed in that very hour. (See verse 13.) When Jesus opened His mouth, the Word proceeded from the Father and created life, for Jesus had said, *"It is the Spirit who gives life.… The words that I speak to you are spirit, and they are life"* (John 6:63). He said, *"I do nothing of Myself; but as My Father taught Me, I speak these things"* (John 8:28), and again, *"For I have not spoken on My own authority; but the Father who sent Me gave Me a command, what I should say and what I should speak"* (John 12:49). No wonder those who heard Him were astonished, for His Word was with power (see Luke 4:32) and He taught as One who had authority (see Mark 1:22). He manifested the authority of the almighty Creator, for he was the *Logos*—the manifested Word of God.

AS THE HOLY SPIRIT SPOKE THROUGH JESUS, SO AFTER THE RESURRECTION, IT IS GOD'S PLAN THAT THIS SAME SPIRIT SHALL NOW SPEAK HIS WORD THROUGH OUR LIPS OF CLAY, TO BRING TO FRUITION THE SAME LIFE-GIVING PLAN AS WAS MINISTERED BY JESUS IN HIS EARTHLY BODY.

This *same Word* is that which God puts into the mouths of every Holy Spirit-baptized believer, and when we speak, it is a manifestation of *glossolalia*—the *Logos*.

No wonder Satan fights tongues!

Jesus demonstrated this new dimension of divine authority and power, but He desired that His body, the church, should also have and use this power and authority, and so He promised to send *"another Helper"* (John 14:16), who would be *in us* (see verse 17) and guide us *"into all truth; for He* [the Holy Spirit] *will not speak on His own authority, but whatever He hears He will speak"* (John 16:13). Here is an amazing truth: when the Comforter, the Holy Spirit, comes into us, He receives the word—the *Logos*—from Jesus, and speaks it through us! As the Holy Spirit spoke through Jesus, so after the resurrection, it is God's plan that this same Spirit shall now speak His word through our lips of clay, to bring to fruition the same life-giving plan as was ministered by Jesus in His earthly body. Our bodies become His body! His words are spoken by us and through us. Oracles of God!

When we speak in tongues, interpret, or prophesy, we do so with words that come from heaven. They are not our words, but we speak them. They are not our thoughts, but they proceed from the Father to accomplish the purpose for which they were sent. We are channels only.

A good analogy is that of a telephone radio repeater station. These have been installed in remote areas in Canada by the Bell Telephone Company to receive and retransmit telephone conversations. On one side of the high tower is a receiver that picks up the voice coming from a transmitter situated on a tower many miles away. This is then amplified and passed into the transmitter on the same tower, and retransmitted to another receiver on another high tower many miles further on. In no case does any operator interpose his thoughts or words into the telephone conversation. The repeater station only speaks what it hears.

We are God's repeater stations on earth, to relay the good news of the gospel of the kingdom heard from heaven, and spoken in the power of the Spirit on earth.

2

TONGUES

When Jesus was obedient to His Father and associated Himself with sinful mankind at His baptism, He chose a son of Adam, John the Baptist, to baptize Him, the Son of God. Thus did He show that sinful man can identify himself with God in this form of burial and resurrection enacted in water baptism. When Jesus came up out of the water, the Spirit of God descended upon Him; the *third* Person descended upon the *second* Person, being sent of the *first* Person, and the result of this anointing by the Spirit was that the Word was heard from heaven, *"This is My beloved Son, in whom I am well pleased"* (Matthew 3:17). Immediately, the spoken word was sent forth from heaven to glorify the Son, which is the ministry of the Holy Spirit. It was a supernatural Word. It came in the power of the Spirit, and immediately Jesus—the incarnate Word of God—began His amazing three-and-a-half years of supernatural ministry. It was said of Him, *"No man ever spoke like this Man!… For He taught them as one having authority, and not as the scribes"* (John 7:46; Matthew 7:29). This was the Word that was released from heaven by the coming of the Holy Spirit on that eventful day. Man, in the person of John, had his part, and Jesus, the Son of God, had His part. So today, God calls man to cooperate in the amazing experience that is called "the baptism in the Spirit," when the Word of God is heard as tongues or languages (*glossolalia*).

To help overcome our unbelief, God seems to have ordered it that we should speak in other tongues or languages. This is not ecstatic gibberish, as some unbelieving people have suggested, but tongues of men or angels. If we were immediately to commence to prophesy in our known tongues, Satan would immediately counter it by telling us that were speaking out of our mind; but when we speak in unlearned tongues, we must be speaking by the Holy Spirit. This is received via our spirit and so bypasses our mind. In our book, *Dominion over Demons*, we have explained that demons may also speak in tongues through people in spiritist séances, but this is outside of the scope of this book. By the pleading or honoring of the blood of Jesus in our prayer for the Holy Spirit baptism, we shall begin to speak in tongues as the Holy Spirit gives us utterance, as He did on the day of Pentecost.

Speaking in tongues supernaturally given is a prophetical oracular utterance from heaven. It is not of man, nor of the wisdom of men, but of God, who knows all languages—past, present, and angelic. He can give any language to His servants if they open their spirits to Him.

Objection is frequently made that many members of the historic or fundamental churches are already "filled with the Spirit" and they have no need of receiving this "embarrassing" tongues experience. It is true that John the Baptist was full of the Spirit from his mother's womb. It is also true that Anna the prophetess was full of the Spirit. Simeon and Zacharias were likewise filled, and it seems quite clear that Elizabeth and Mary the mother of Jesus were filled "right up to the top." All this was *before Pentecost*. At Pentecost, they were not only filled, but they overflowed. Jesus has said, "*Out of* [your] *heart will flow rivers of living water*" (John 7:38). He was not thinking of a pool, however refreshing, but of springs of water, rivers of water, fountains springing up in the desert all around us.

A good analogy is that of a sponge. A dry sponge is useless, and many church going people are dry sponges today. A little of the Holy Spirit in their lives and these people can become damp—some damper than others, and some even become saturated, i.e. filled so full that no more water can be absorbed. Take this saturated sponge and plunge (baptize, in Greek, *baptizo*—immerse) into water and the saturated sponge becomes super-saturated and overflows from every hole and pore. It is this overflowing of the Spirit that produces the *Logos*, the Word, flowing in the power of the Spirit. This is analogous to the baptism in the Spirit. When, as an act of free will, we turn on the faucet or tap of our human tongues, the flow of living water from the illimitable reservoir flows out of our mouths as the life-giving Word of God. Jesus said, "*The words that I speak to you are spirit, and they are life*" (John 6:63). These words can create life, destroy death and sickness, and cast the devil out of lives and situations. Jesus cast out demons with the Word of God. (See Matthew 8:16.) We also cast out demons and heal the sick today by the same Word.

There are seven major usages of tongues:

1. FOR PERSONAL EDIFICATION

"*He who speaks in a tongue edifies himself*" (1 Corinthians 14:4). We must always remember that in the Spirit he will be speaking mysteries. Man has invented many palliatives—pills, potions, drugs, heating pads, drink, cigarettes, pep pills, etc., ad infinitum. But when a Holy Spirit-baptized believer turns on the valve that brings forth the water of life from heaven, he refreshes himself so intensely, and washes away the cobwebs and the blues and the pains, that recourse to the means of man becomes unnecessary, and the resultant joy and ecstasy must be experienced to be understood. One with the experience is not at the mercy of one with an argument against it.

2. FOR PRAISE

Praising God in tongues will cause depression, despondency, and despair—the three Ds of the devil—to disappear. Praise is natural to a person released from Satanic bondages, and Paul told us that it is possible (and desirable) to praise *"with the Spirit"* as well as *"with the understanding"* (1 Corinthians 14:14–15). A burst of tongues of praise to God will bring one up from the depths to the heights, always remembering that the Word of God teaches us that we are in heavenly places in Christ. This is the Christian's position. When we join our tongues in praise with the tongues of heaven and angels, we find that this statement is true. *We are* in heavenly places in Christ. The expressions "Hallelujah" and "Glory to God" become natural expressions.

3. FOR SINGING

We have often heard people baptized in the Spirit begin by speaking in tongues, and then proceed into spiritual song, with tunes and words received direct from heaven. On one occasion we were staying in the home of a Lutheran Pastor in Colombia, South America, and it was arranged that we should pray for his wife to receive her personal Pentecost, he having already received. Very soon, she was in "heavenly places" and speaking in tongues, and then, after a few minutes, she went from speaking to singing, and four of us present all joined in—and a heavenly choir was heard on the earth. We believe it is in God's plan in His church that both singing with the understanding and singing in the Spirit should take place in all local assemblies.

4. FOR PRAYER

Oh, how many have agonized in prayer without this blessed baptism in the Spirit! In Romans 8:26, it is written, *"Likewise the Spirit also helps in our weaknesses. For we do not know what we should pray for as we ought, but the Spirit Himself makes intercession for us with groanings which cannot be uttered."* It is when we have a deep need in prayer that the Spirit of God helps us in our human weaknesses. We know not how to frame our thoughts into words, we only groan with groanings that are uttered, but turn on that valve and the Spirit will begin to pray for us, and our prayers will be answered. We shall feel the burden lift and peace will reign in our hearts. For intercessory prayer, "praying in the Spirit" is a necessity, and God has provided us with this weapon in the power of the Spirit. By this means, we can also obey God's Word and *"pray without ceasing"* (1 Thessalonians 5:17), we can pray as we work!

5. FOR REBUKING EVIL SPIRITS

The ministry of casting out of demons, and the strong prayer of faith that liberates the oppressed in mind and body, is now returning to the church. A most cogent method of attacking demon's powers is to rebuke them in tongues. Evil spirits cannot stand this frontal attack, and will be glad to be cast out of a person rather than listen to a heavenly language spoken by a believer in the power of the Spirit. It stirs them up, and if used in conjunction with pleading the blood of Jesus out loud, lays an artillery barrage that weakens the demon's powers. Remember always that the manifestation of tongues is the manifestation of the living Word, Jesus Himself, proceeding out of our mouths like a two-edged sword. (See Revelation 19:15.) The more faith we put into the utterance, the more Satan will crumble up in his defenses and flee.

6. FOR SPEAKING IN THE TONGUE OF ONE WHO UNDERSTANDS

The experience on the Day of Pentecost is frequently duplicated in our day, when Jews from sixteen surrounding nations understood the tongues spoken by the 120. (See Acts 2:4.) They understood in the tongues wherein they were born. To quote a case in recent times, we heard Rev. Harald Bredesen, a Reformed Church Minister from Mount Vernon, New York, testify that he spoke in tongues in the lobby of a New York City hotel and was understood by an Egyptian lady sitting nearby. Harald Bredesen did not know this woman, but he was impelled to speak, as prompted by the Holy Spirit. This woman explained that he had spoken in high archaic Egyptian only possible in certain Egyptian universities. She was most intrigued to know how he could have told her of her past history in this language. He at once opened his Bible and showed her the relevant passages, and it is believed that she was greatly moved to accept Christ as her Savior by this act of the Holy Spirit through human lips. Cases of this type can be multiplied where languages unknown to the speaker have been understood by another listener, who has often been won to Christ, for the Holy Spirit always glorifies the Christ.

7. FOR USE IN THE CHURCH

The time for personal prayer and edification must come to an end when we enter the church. Now we are members of one body, coming together to manifest Jesus the Word corporately. The gifts of the Spirit are to be used in the church for the edification of the church members. The time of personal edification should have taken place at home, before coming to church, so that we are prayed up and full of the joy of the Lord. We should not go to church to "get a lift," but rather to "give a lift." The church is the place where we give forth in the power of the Spirit. Thus, we are instructed not to speak in tongues out loud unless we know there is a person with the second gift of interpretation present. If we know or believe there is no such gift in a particular assembly, then Paul instructed us to speak to ourselves and to God (see 1 Corinthians 14:28), quietly and reverently, for the Holy Spirit is gentle and will never startle or cause confusion in a worship service. Such disturbing occurrences must be influenced by other spirits.

A person able to speak in tongues for private use should wait on the Lord to be enabled to exercise a tongue for the purpose of bringing forth an interpretation for the edification of the whole church, for we must be zealous of these charismata that we may excel to the edifying of the church. (See 1 Corinthians 14:12.) When one possesses a clear tongue, it should be spoken out clearly, distinctly, reverently, without shouting, gesticulating, or using a high pitched or hysterical voice. Such a tongue must not be mumbled. If it is not possible for a person to bring forth the gift of tongues in the church in this clear, convincing manner, then it would be better to keep silence and continue to wait on God until it becomes possible. If the church is to be edified, unbelievers must be convinced by the very way this gift is used. They will then be in awe of Him. (See 1 Corinthians 14:25.)

This is what was meant by Paul when he wrote, *"Do all have gifts of healings? Do all speak with tongues? Do all interpret?"* (1 Corinthians 12:30). This is the ministration of a particular charismatic gift for the edification of the church. It is quite obvious that although all may speak in tongues for personal edification, yet all do not speak in tongues to edify the church, nor do they all interpret or pray for the sick. Satan has prevented thousands from receiving the gift of tongues from a wrong twisted interpretation of this Scripture. May he suffer in eternity for this grievous misrepresentation!

3

THE PROPHETICAL WORD

In the last chapter we discussed the purpose of *glossolalia*, the initial manifestation of "prophecy." God greatly desires that the church, which is His body, should be fed by the living Word, bread from heaven, which the manna typified in the Old Testament. Not only do we have the written canon of Scripture, but in the plan of God, He desires to confirm this Word by speaking audibly to His people, thereby the Holy Spirit becomes a Guide and Teacher.

By the three oral gifts of tongues, interpretation, and prophecy, God's *voice* is heard in our day. It seems that the single charismatic gift of prophecy is confined to *edification, exhortation,* and *comfort.* (See 1 Corinthians 14:3.) In every worship service in church, the voice of God should be heard in this gift edifying the body, exhorting to holier living, deeper consecration, and stirring it up to bring others under the sound of the gospel. There will always be those who are sorrowing or grieving, and God will speak directly to them in their sorrows with words of comfort. How necessary is this gift in the church!

Where the gift of tongues is used in the assembly to bring forth the Word in interpretation, the manifestation of this twin gift is equivalent to the single utterance of prophecy. Where a prayer meeting is held for believers only, it would seem that the use of tongues was in some measure unnecessary, for the gift of prophecy may be used by several members. *"Let the prophets speak two or three, and let the other judge"* (1 Corinthians 14:29). Where unbelievers are present, or those who have not come under the teaching of the need of the baptism of the Spirit and the gifts, then the use of tongues plus interpretation is most desirable, and it would appear that this method has divine approval, for it is written, *"Therefore tongues are for a sign, not to those who believe but to unbelievers"* (1 Corinthians 14:22). It is not possible to overestimate the tremendous impact that speaking in tongues has upon an unbelieving ear. We have seen people rush out of church when a well-modulated tongue has been used!

Interpretation of tongues, which is the twin of the gift of tongues, is only used following the manifestation of glossolalia in the church, where such a tongue has been used for this purpose. Interpretation is not transliteration, but rather giving forth the message that has already been spoken in an unknown tongue. The person giving forth the tongue may have spoken few words, but the interpretation may be many words, but the sense will be received by the listening members of the church. Practice makes perfect in the use of these gifts, as in other things of life; they are not automatically spoken, but the human vessel cooperates with the divine Word to bring it forth under a strong anointing of the Spirit. Some have not become expert, and so do not know when the meaning of the message has ceased, and will sometimes repeat themselves in slightly different ways, like a phonograph record repeating itself. God never takes away the human responsibility, for *"the spirits of the prophets are subject to the prophets"* (1 Corinthians 14:32), which means that we use our free will, and stop and start at will, which disposes of the ridiculous claim made by many untutored people that "the Holy Spirit made them" speak, usually out of place. The Holy Spirit does not force us to do anything.

We prophesy according to the proportion of our faith. (See Romans 12:6.) Some have more faith than others in this gift, and will usually bring forth a deeper word. If faith is weak, or the anointing not strong, it is possible for the human mind to intrude some of its own thoughts, and so the prophetical utterance will be partly of the Holy Spirit and partly of the mind of man, even if that mind is a sanctified mind. In fact, some "prophecies" are simply a sanctified mind giving forth a truth already learned. What is said may be true, and possibly edify, but great care has to be taken that personal opinions or instructions are avoided. It is good to remember the confines of this particular gift—edification, exhortation, and comfort—not fortune telling or instruction given to any member of the church! Practice makes perfect!

THE APOSTLE PAUL CLEARLY TAUGHT US THAT WE MUST NOT DESPISE PROPHESY, NOR QUENCH THE SPIRIT, BUT WE MUST ENCOURAGE THE USE OF THESE GIFTS, AND THEN DELIBERATELY *PROVE* THE WORD SPOKEN, AND APPLY IT, IF WE CAN, TO OURSELVES, BUT NEVER TO ANOTHER!

When it is realized that mistakes can be made in the prophetical gift, some get greatly discouraged, and therefore have no confidence in the Word spoken; but this is a great mistake, for the apostle Paul clearly taught us that we must not despise prophesy, nor quench the Spirit, but we must encourage the use of these gifts, and then deliberately *prove* the Word spoken, and apply it, if we can, to ourselves, but never to another! Some assemblies have thrown out all the gifts of the Spirit, because some unruly members, who were unteachable, have misused these gifts. We must never quench the Spirit, or the utterances of the Spirit, but must teach our assemblies how to use them, for the Bible teaching is quite clear. Pastors must be bold and instruct and correct misuse where necessary.

Not all prophetic words spoken are of necessity "interpretation" when following a tongue. Sometimes, members of the church may not have a ministry of tongues to the church, but may burst forth in ecstatic praise and worship, which may well be followed by a prophetical utterance. At other times, tongues are sometimes used to trigger off a prophetical utterance, because the speaker desires to be in the Spirit as much as possible, and to keep the human mind silent. A "burst of tongues," followed by a prophetical utterance, will not be "tongues plus interpretation," but prophecy launched by tongues! It seems clear from Paul's teachings that it is unwise to speak in tongues and then endeavor immediately afterward to interpret one's own tongue. *"If anyone speaks in a tongue…let one interpret"* (1 Corinthians 14:27). The context would seem to indicate that if there be no interpreter present, one should speak in tongues quietly to God, but conversely, if one has a gift of tongues, then prayer should be made that the second gift of interpretation be given so that the church might be edified.

God might overrule, however, in all these instances.

In all utterance gifts, we need to remember that all things must be done decently and in order. (See 1 Corinthians 14:40.) Confusion, disorder, and interruptions must be avoided if the unbelieving are to be convinced. Unruly members will sometimes interpret the sermon, and say "God told them to do so!" These people must be taught and disciplined if necessary. Similarly, when a call is made to the unsaved, great care must be taken if it is felt to be God's will to bring forth an encouraging Word to the unsaved.

In the Old Testament, schools of prophets were held, which would seem to be the ancient counterpart of Bible schools or theological seminaries. Here, young men were trained in giving forth the supernatural word, and we believe our churches should similarly be places where members are trained in the voice gifts. Obadiah took a hundred prophets and hid them, fifty in a cave, and fed them during the persecutions in the time of Jezebel and Ahab. (See 1 Kings 18:4.) Before his translation, Elijah visited schools in Gilgal, Bethel, and Jericho. It was during the building of a new school residence that the axe head was made to swim. (See 2 Kings 4:40–41.)

Great skill has to be used by prophets in the church, and it seems there are three degrees of this utterance gift. First, the ministry of a prophet to the church. This ministry gift is usually associated with the apostolic ministry, for these two offices seemed to work as a two-witness ministry to the early church. It would therefore be expected that when an apostle and prophet visited an assembly the Word would be brought forth richly and in great power. In local assemblies, prophetesses were frequently great assets to the church, for Philip had four daughters who prophesied at Caesarea. (See Acts 21:9.) In this case, a local church can have a local prophetical ministry, and the members of this church will develop confidence in the prophetical utterances spoken by these chosen vessels, male or female. As the testimony of Jesus is the spirit of prophecy (see Revelation 19:10), it is not surprising that any member who is baptized in the Spirit may be moved upon under special circumstances to prophesy in the church. If these utterances are brought forth in the assembly, we must encourage the users to go on with God, so that the supply of prophets or prophetesses shall increase and not dry up!

If a prophecy is heard that condemns certain members (or the pastor) they must not be accepted as of the Spirit of God, but must be suppressed, for *"there is therefore now no condemnation to those who are in Christ Jesus"* (Romans 8:1). It is certain that the person concerned has a wrong spirit, and if necessary must confess it and deliverance must be prayed for before any further utterance can be trusted. Jesus gave us His yardstick—*"You will know them by their fruits"* (Matthew 7:16). Anyone not manifesting the fruits of the spirit, or living in some sinful state, should, under no circumstances, be permitted to speak in the church.

When King Saul backslid, God permitted a lying spirit to come upon him, and he prophesied by the lying spirit, although previously he had prophesied by the Holy Spirit. Later, the Spirit of God came upon Saul again when he repented, but again he backslid and finally became possessed of the lying spirit, which finally drove him to the witch of Endor, and then to his destruction. Great care must be taken that we do not permit evil spirits to utter their prophecies out of the unsanctified minds of backsliding Christians.

It will be obvious that the gift of the discerning of spirits must be in every church, especially in the pastor.

One of the ascension gifts of Christ to the church is a pastor. The ideal of a New Testament pastor is one who has a great knowledge of the Bible and is filled with the Spirit and possesses the charismatic gifts of the Spirit. By the gifts of discerning of spirits and the word of knowledge, he will be able to know what he is dealing with, and in the love of Christ, but in the power of the Spirit, he must discipline and teach those over whom the Lord has made him the overseer! (See Acts 20:28). The conception that an assembly may hire or fire a pastor is alien to Scripture and the Spirit of God. In fact, we are instructed to give the pastor double honor. The body of Christ is not a democracy but a theocracy, ruled by Jesus through the Holy Spirit, through His five-fold ministry of apostles, prophets, pastors, evangelists, and teachers. These are God's gifts to the church for the blessing of the body of Christ.

4

THE WORD OF POWER

Immediately following the anointing of the Holy Spirit upon Jesus at His baptism, as described in Luke 4, we read that *"Jesus returned **in the power of the Spirit**"* (verse 14). Like an arrow from the bow of God, He returned to the very place, Nazareth, where He had been brought up, where He was well known, and where He had always worshipped as a young man. No one knew who He really was before His anointing with the Spirit, and likewise no one knew who He was that day when He entered His own synagogue. He was just a local man, a son of Joseph the carpenter. In like manner, those who are beginning to manifest the *Logos* of power are not recognized today by the church leaders or congregations of our cities. There was a difference this day, however, for the *Logos* of God had been anointed by the coming of the Spirit, and when Jesus entered the synagogue He was granted permission to read from their sacred scrolls, and quoted from the very Scriptures that spoke of Himself, and the reason for His anointing: to preach, to heal, to open, to deliver, to set at liberty, and to give sight to the blind. This needed a power that the Jewish clergy did not possess. He preached to them a little sermon, and told them that *"no prophet* [was] *accepted in his own country"* (Luke 4:24), and true to form they manhandled Him, leading Him out of the city, and tried to throw Him over a cliff—all because He came to deliver them in spirit, soul, and body. They did not want deliverance, or to be shown a better way. They wanted no competition from an ignorant carpenter's son; He was not of their priestly class or training.

He then entered into Capernaum and they were astonished at His doctrine, *"for His word was authority"* (verse 32). As no one knew Him in Nazareth, so in Capernaum; He was just a Jew, a carpenter, certainly not a priest! How wrong could they be? He was the High Priest from heaven! He was the King of Kings. He was the chief Apostle and Prophet. He was all these offices, rolled into one. He was the living *Logos*, the Word made flesh. (See John 1:14.) When He opened His mouth that His Father had filled, they were amazed, for His Word was *power*.

The only living creatures that recognized Him were demons! Demons in the synagogue; unclean spirits recognized Him as Jesus of Nazareth, the Holy One of God. (See Luke 4:34.) They were afraid of His Word, and immediately they spoke. Jesus spoke and manifest the *Logos* and they fled from His Word of power. This manifestation of God's living Word produced such consternation in Satan's kingdom that the demons were unable to hold their peace and kept crying out through the mouths of people as they came out, *"You are the Christ, the Son of God"* (John 11:27). The Word manifest in the flesh only had to appear and to speak, and demons came out crying with loud voices, naming themselves and acknowledging His Messiahship. The same happens today!

No wonder they said, *"What a word this is!"* (Luke 4:36).

There are three *power* gifts of the Spirit that are given to the body of Christ to manifest the Word of power to do the same work as Jesus did in healing the sick, casting out demons, and cleansing the lepers. These words of power must be "prophesied," that is, spoken forth by human lips in the power of the Spirit as divine oracular utterances, against

Satan and his cohorts. If this is done in faith, then we shall see the same results today as they saw in the synagogue at Capernaum!

The apostle Paul told us to seek the "best gifts." We believe that the power gifts are certainly in this category, for whereas the three oral gifts are given to edify, to comfort, and to stir up, the power gifts are what we use after we have been edified and prepared. We go into battle encouraged from the exhortations and briefings given by the Holy Spirit. We start to preach and proclaim the meaning of Calvary and the complete defeat of Satan; we show forth the Word of power, which brings us head-on into conflict with demonic powers.

WE GO INTO BATTLE ENCOURAGED FROM THE
EXHORTATIONS AND BRIEFINGS GIVEN BY
THE HOLY SPIRIT. WE START TO PREACH AND
PROCLAIM THE MEANING OF CALVARY AND
THE COMPLETE DEFEAT OF SATAN;
WE SHOW FORTH THE WORD OF POWER,
WHICH BRINGS US HEAD-ON INTO CONFLICT
WITH DEMONIC POWERS.

We heard one Anglican pastor testify that he had known nothing about demons, and certainly did not realize their presence, until *after* he received the baptism in the Spirit and spoke in tongues. This began the flowing forth from him of the river of life, the *Logos* of God, and Satan will cry out against such ministry, sometimes with a loud voice! There is only one thing to do, to rebuke with this Word of power and cast him out and tread him under foot. This will certainly astonish, and will bring considerable opposition as well as joy, but this is what God is bringing us into today in this last day revelation of the *Logos* of God.

In Joel 2:11, it is written, "*The LORD **gives voice** before His army… for **strong** is the One who executes **His word**.*" Before the army of the Lord, the Holy Spirit-anointed church—His true body—is prepared to go into the final battle of the ages against sin, sickness, suffering, and sorrow, it will be necessary for the *voice* gifts to be restored and used in the power of the Spirit. Thus, today we are seeing a restoration of the power charismatic gifts, which are healing people of all known diseases, driving out demons, and delivering people from the cruel bondages of Satan. Jesus used this Word of power at the tomb of Lazarus. Just three words were necessary and life came back into a corrupting human body.

What a word is this!

Jesus showed us how to pray for the sick. He stood *over* Peter's mother-in-law, who had a high fever, rebuked it, and it left her, proving that fever has intelligence! He told His disciples to cast mountains into the seas, providing they did not doubt in their hearts. This could only be done by the Word of faith, which He told them to have, and which is always given to heal a sick person or do a miraculous work. (See Luke 11:22–24.) He taught His disciples to take dominion over the circumstance and cast it away violently with the faith of God! The apostle James instructed the elders of the church to pray over the sick, not to pray a pious hopeful prayer for them, but to take the initiative and dominion and to cast out the sickness and cast away the mountain! Cancers are indeed mountains to those who have them. We need to speak as those with authority.

These three *power* gifts of *faith*, *miracles*, and *healings* manifest the Word of power in action—*Jesus*, in action through the members of His body. This mouth of ours was not given for cursing, grumbling, or confessing failure, but to be used as an orifice through which God's power could flow to cause devilish things to disintegrate and disappear. Thus, we address ourselves to sicknesses, to demons, and to circumstances: "In the name of Jesus, I *command* you to go." Remember Jesus said, "[If you do] *not doubt not in* [your] *heart*…[you] *will have whatever* [**you**] *say"* (Mark 11:23).

This is the prayer of faith. It is a "saying prayer." The saying, with "no doubt in our hearts," is the manifestation of prophecy in the form of *powerful words* against which Satan cannot stand.

When these words are spoken by more and more anointed men and women today, Satan's kingdom will be invaded by the army of the Lord, and His army is very great. Satan may scheme and plan for the overthrow of the kingdom of God; he may plot to take over the world by communism, and to kill Christians with sicknesses or drive them into mental hospitals, but his day is ending. The Lord's army is great and terrible; the *Logos* of God is proceeding out of thousands of mouths as this army enters Satan's territory with banners flying. Consternation will be seen on the faces of Satan's army of demon spirits. They will flee in every direction in confusion, vacating lives that they have held in captivity for centuries. Jesus, the living Word of God, was manifest that He might open prison doors and set the captives free. This is the day of the church. This is why it was created at Pentecost by the coming of the Holy Spirit. This is the *"acceptable year of the* Lord*"* (Luke 4:19).

5

THE WORD OF REVELATION

As we have already explained, the original coming of the Holy Spirit in power upon the church on the day of Pentecost was accompanied by an effusion of tongues, which Peter likened to "prophecy." This effusion is not confined to glossolalia, but to nine particular manifestations of the prophetical utterance called "spirituals" (in Greek, *pneumatikos*) or gifts (in Greek, *charismata*). In both these words, we have the thought conveyed that these gifts are for the purpose of showing forth the love of Jesus in the power of the Spirit; in fact, they are the many facets of the ministry of Jesus shining forth from His anointed body.

The three revelation gifts of the word of knowledge, the word of wisdom, and the discerning of spirits are to enable the warrior Christian in the army of the Lord, to have revealed to him secrets by a word from *the Logos* of God. Thus, the Holy Spirit is able to make known things that are unknown to unanointed men and women. These three gifts should only be used by Christians who are very experienced in the ministry of the gifts of the Spirit, for they are so high and heady, as the best of the best gifts, that Satan can easily attack in this area. The word of knowledge will reveal the secrets of men's hearts (see 1 Corinthians 14:25) including their intentions, their thoughts, their sicknesses, and the causes of these things. Such knowledge is not for broadcasting, but in order that we might know how to help such people. This gift also includes foretelling things to come, which is sometimes called the gift of prophecy, but as we have shown, this gift is deeper than the prophetical gift in the church. This is a ministry that is more likely to be used by a prophet in the church. Again, we repeat that these gifts in the hands, or mouths, of a non-humble person can be spiritual dynamite to wreck a person's life! They are not fortune telling gifts. The gift of fortune telling belongs to the demon world, and we must be most careful about inquiring of demons. (See Isaiah 8:19–20.) Jesus told them to hold their peace and come out.

It is quite usual that where God permits us to have a word of knowledge on any matter whatsoever, He will, at the same time, give us a word of wisdom to go along with the revealed knowledge. This will enable us to give divine guidance to one in need of it, and sometimes, a sufferer does not know what ails them, or the reasons for it, but the gifts reveal this and the Holy Spirit will usually confirm the revelation to the afflicted one, and so faith rises and it is possible to deliver the person.

Great care must be taken that before a word can be accepted as from the Lord Himself, the vessel through whom such a word is given is known to have such a prophetical ministry that has brought great blessing to others. Such a man or woman must be held in great love and esteem for their work in the ministry; it is not sufficient that any person claiming to be a prophet shall hand out guidance and counsel, for many false prophets have gone out into the world. We would again mention that God has a law—*"by the mouth of two or three witnesses every word shall be established"* (2 Corinthians 13:1). In matters of personal guidance, it is prudent to receive similar words of guidance and wisdom from at least two trusted servants of God, which is why the Lord caused apostles and prophets to go in pairs when establishing New Testament churches! He wants us to be as wise as serpents and harmless as doves.

In the same way, as we are not to believe any doctrine of Scripture unless it is confirmed out of the mouths of two writers, so also no revelation of the spoken Logos shall be believed without confirmatory witnesses.

The responsibility of action taken after the Word of guidance is given rests with the one who receives it, not the ones who give it. Paul was warned not to go to Jerusalem because bonds awaited him, and he heard this confirmed in every city, but he decided to go in spite of the Spirit-given warning, and he was bound when he got there! The wisdom given to the apostleship overrode the warning counsel in the gifts.

Beware of freelance prophets!

IN MATTERS OF PERSONAL GUIDANCE, IT IS PRUDENT TO RECEIVE SIMILAR WORDS OF GUIDANCE AND WISDOM FROM AT LEAST TWO TRUSTED SERVANTS OF GOD, WHICH IS WHY THE LORD CAUSED APOSTLES AND PROPHETS TO GO IN PAIRS WHEN ESTABLISHING NEW TESTAMENT CHURCHES! HE WANTS US TO BE AS WISE AS SERPENTS AND HARMLESS AS DOVES.

One of the most common ways to test a false prophet is to check their message. If the prophesy is that you will receive a ministry of great importance, and the flesh of man loves to hear this kind of thing, then their utterance is suspect. Try the spirits and see if they are of God. If a personal prophecy unveils events of great importance that will bring glory to the Lord and His work, and cause us to cast ourselves prostrate at His feet, we can then ask God to fulfill it His way in our lives, while we prepare ourselves to be so used for His glory and honor.

So many prophecies given seem contradictory. Consider the words predicting that Jesus would be born in Bethlehem, yet He would be of Nazareth and yet come out of Egypt! How could this be from God? It is safe to let God work out His own prophecies, for Jesus said, *"I have told you before it comes, that when it does come to pass, **you may believe!**"* (John 14:29). What goes for prophetical utterances in our day also goes for prophecies of the Bible yet unfulfilled. Let us not guess how God is going to do it!

In his prison cell, Joseph heard many wonderful prophecies concerning himself and his future ministry, and it is recorded that *"the word of the LORD tested him"* (Psalm 105:19). Many nights he went to sleep in bonds, wondering how the impossible could become the possible. His promises were fulfilled to a far greater degree than he could ever understand or imagine. He allowed himself to be tried by the prophetical word.

Remember too that a prophetical Word will never go past the written Word of God. The two must agree. John wrote that *"the Father, the **Word**, and the Holy Spirit all agree in one"* (1 John 5:7 KJV). The written Word of God is the final authority, and the means whereby we test false utterances. If such prophecies are heard in your church, the pastor should lovingly but firmly counsel the "prophet." If they will hear, they will have a humble spirit, but if not, it shows they are false, for they have a proud spirit, which God hates. Not only should we not receive such prophecies, but the speaker also should be instructed to remain silent, in the name of the Lord, for it is of another spirit.

In cases of difficulty when a word is not understood by a member of a church, he or she should take such a word to the pastor, who will seek the understanding from God by a word of wisdom, or, better still, take it to several men of God who are known to be *experienced* in the use of spiritual gifts. *"Let **two** or **three** prophets speak, and let the others judge"* (1 Corinthians 14:29). The men of God can speak wisdom, but you will have to judge! It is obvious that one who does not regularly use a prophetical gift will not be able to help in cases of difficulties or misunderstandings.

If a single individual comes to you and says, "I have a word from the Lord for you," listen to it with respect, and apply all the above tests to it. It might be of God, or it might be from a proud human spirit giving way to a lying spirit, but let us be careful not to make the easy mistake of despising prophesyings, against which we are warned. (See 1 Thessalonians 5:20–21.) Receive everything, test and prove everything, and *hold fast* to that which is proved to be good. If it is of God, it will happen and you will be blessed. If it is not of God, it will not come to pass anyway, and the prophet will be proved a liar, which is the test of a prophet in the Bible. *"When a prophet speaks in the name of the LORD, if the thing does not happen or come to pass, that is the thing which the LORD has not spoken; the prophet has spoken it presumptuously; you shall not be afraid of him"* (Deuteronomy 18:22).

Do not turn away from the greater gifts of revelation, for they are in the church for the purpose of causing it to win the great battle of the ages, the defeat of Satan's kingdom, and the bringing in of the kingdom of God's dear Son.

Many who begin to get the first manifestations of these revelation gifts, especially the gift of discerning of spirits, often get greatly troubled, because in "seeing through" a person, they think they are judging them, and of course judgment belongs to God. To know is not to judge in a condemnatory sense. We have the mind of Christ, and will realize this supernatural knowledge in a greater degree in the day in which we are living. God wishes to warn us sometimes that we are speaking to a wolf in sheep's clothing, a false prophet in the church, a deceitful worker of iniquity masquerading as a child of God. *"From among yourselves men will rise up, speaking perverse things, to draw away the disciples after themselves"* (Acts 20:30).

God does not want us to be fooled. The most common form of deception is from alcoholics and drug addicts who want a hand out from kind-hearted Christians, not for food or bed, but for more drink, cigarettes, or drugs. Do not give them money, but offer food. both natural and spiritual; they will almost certainly refuse both! Their stories will tear the heart out of a tender Christian, but the revelation gifts will show us they are not often genuine. Ask God to reveal to you their true state before you are unwise in enabling addicts in their addiction!

6

THE RETURN OF ELIJAH

In the last chapter of the Old Testament, it is very significant that New Testament revival is prophesied by Malachi:

> *Behold, I will send you Elijah the prophet* **before** *the coming of the great and dreadful day of the* LORD. *And he will turn the hearts of the fathers to the children, and the hearts of the children to their fathers, lest I come and strike the earth with a curse.*
>
> (Malachi 4:5–6)

This "Elijah ministry" is obviously a restoration ministry to save the world from judgment. If there was ever a day that Satan under God could curse this old world, it is today, but God has prophesied that He will send *"Elijah the prophet"* to stem the tide of iniquity, to reverse it, and to restore righteousness. Today is either a day of destruction or recreation. There is no middle ground.

The name *Elijah* means "God Himself," or "The Lord is *God*." When the prophet Elijah came suddenly upon a backslidden Israel in the time of wicked King Ahab and his idolatrous Queen Jezebel, he was a manifestation of Jehovah in the flesh. He was a type of Emmanuel, the greater Elijah yet to come. What he prophesied came to pass; he both shut up heaven and opened it again. He turned off the rain and turned on the rain. This is a major result of the prophetical ministry today. We can bind and loose on earth, and God in heaven will answer our commands! This is the power of the *spoken word* given in faith. This is the word that breaks in pieces the rock. It is a *hammer* and a *sword*.

God Himself was manifest to a completely wayward and backslidden Israel and in *one day* the people chose unanimously to serve God. The revival was rapid and caused by the prophetical words spoken by Elijah. "*When all the people saw it, they fell on their faces; and they said, 'The Lord, He is God! The Lord, He is God!'*" (1 Kings 18:39).

Elijah's prayer before the fire came down from heaven was a short prayer; he did not shout, stamp his foot, look pious, or try to be important; he prayed the prayer of faith—just sixty-three words, and asked God to send fire from heaven according to *His word*. (See 1 Kings 18:36–37.) Without any hesitation, we read, "*Then the fire of the Lord fell*" (1 Kings 18:38).

The Spirit of Jehovah that was in Jesus Christ was in Elijah, for the testimony of Jesus is the spirit of prophecy. As God was in Christ manifesting Himself to Israel, so also was God in Elijah to win back Israel to Himself. This is the Elijah ministry. It is a ministry of the prophetical Word to offer reconciliation and to give restoration.

In like manner, God sent John the Baptist in the power and spirit of Elijah to prepare the way for the greater Elijah, Jesus Himself. John was a prophet full of the Holy Spirit from his mother's womb. He spoke the Words of God that prepared the way for the ministry of Jesus. The same spirit that was in Elijah was in John for the same purpose.

But what did you go out to see? …A prophet? Yes, I say to you, and more than a prophet. For this is he of whom it is written: Behold, I send My messenger before Your face, Who will prepare Your way before You. …And if you are willing to receive it, **he is Elijah** *who is to come. He who has ears to hear, let him hear!*

(Matthew 11:8–10, 14–15)

John demonstrated the Elijah ministry in his day.

Obviously, John did not fully fulfill the prophesies of Malachi concerning the coming of Elijah, because all things were not restored by John, but Jesus again reiterated that Elijah would indeed come to restore all things, *"Why then do the scribes say that Elijah must come first?"* (Matthew 17:10). Jesus answered them, *"Indeed, Elijah is coming first come and will* **restore all things***"* (verse 11). This same Spirit that was in Elijah and John the Baptist is yet to restore all things back to God's paradise.

> ## THE ELIJAH MINISTRY THAT GOD IS RAISING UP IN OUR DAY WILL AGAIN INCLUDE THE RESTORATION OF THE APOSTLESHIP AND THE PROPHETICAL MINISTRY IN THE POWER OF THE SPIRIT, FOR THE REVELATION OF THE RESTORATION OF THE NEW TESTAMENT CHURCH CAN ONLY COME THROUGH THE TWIN MINISTRIES OF THE APOSTLE AND PROPHET.

Jesus was a personal fulfillment of all the kings and prophets before Him. He was a greater than Solomon, a greater than Elijah, to *"turn the hearts of the fathers to the children, and the hearts of the children to their fathers"* (Malachi 4:6). Jesus is *God Himself*, the Word made flesh. However, Jesus came and ministered in the power of the Spirit for only three-and-a-half years. The ministry of Elijah did not finish at the cross, but commenced to increase at Pentecost, when the *Logos* came into 120 empty vessels, forming the true body of Christ on earth. Now there were 120 mouths to sound forth the *Logos* instead of one. When Satan silenced the mouth of Jesus, he caused 120 other mouths to be opened; Satan always defeats himself by his actions. These 120 mouths were not a final count, because this great blessing of Pentecost was to go to the uttermost part of the earth. (See Acts 1:8.) In our day, we can expect millions of mouths to be anointed by the Holy Spirit to sound forth Word hammer blows to Satan's kingdom. *"Behold, I have put My words in your mouth"* (Jeremiah 1:9). The same words that were in the mouth of Jesus are now found in the mouths of the members of His Holy Spirit filled body. These words manifest Elijah—God Himself.

The Elijah ministry that God is raising up in our day will again include the restoration of the apostleship and the prophetical ministry in the power of the Spirit, for the revelation of the restoration of the New Testament church can only come through the twin ministries of the apostle and prophet. *"How that by revelation He made known to me the mystery…which in other ages was not made known to the sons of men, as it has **now** been revealed by the Spirit to His holy apostles and prophets"* (Ephesians 3:3, 5). This revealed mystery was that the Gentiles were to be made fellow heirs, and of the same body of Christ, and truly, when the Gentiles were received by God through the Holy Spirit's visitation upon them, they also "spoke with tongues, and magnified God." (See Acts 10:46.) By this manifestation of the *Logos*, God showed the Jews that "repentance unto life was also granted to the Gentiles." (See Acts 11:18.)

The manifestation of the spoken prophetical word brought life to the Gentiles!

As God continues to pour out His Spirit upon all flesh today, and our sons and daughters begin to prophesy, i.e., manifest the gifts of the

Spirit through their lives, so will the Word of God be brought in the power of the Spirit to break down the strongholds of Satan, to open the prison house of those that are bound, to set the captives free, and to build up again the temple of the Holy Spirit, built without hands of living stones of human beings on fire for God. As in Elijah's day, so in ours, "And then the fire fell," for he who came in the Spirit of Elijah prophesied "[Jesus] *will baptize you with the Holy Spirit and fire*" (Matthew 3:11).

The *Logos* is not only a hammer, but it is also burning fire. His ministers shall be a flame of fire. As the members of the historic churches receive this glorious baptism in the Spirit, He will be a Guide and Teacher to them and will lead them into all truth. He will teach them that the purpose of this baptism in the Spirit, accompanied by the effusion of the *Logos*, is not to make them better denominational members, but to bring them into the true temple of the Spirit to reveal Christ the living Word. The leadership will be of the Spirit, it will not be political or repressive; it will not be carnal according to the cunning devices of men's hearts. It will be open and honest for all to see the wonderful works of God. Apostles, prophets, pastors, evangelists and teachers will again be set in this body, and will minister the things of God to the hungry. Thus will Elijah return to restore all things—the church, the nation of Israel, and then the world. The alternative is that the earth shall be smitten with a curse.

Shall we pray that we shall not hinder Elijah—God Himself—in this restoration work? Shall we lend our talents to cooperate and be filled with the Spirit? Thus shall we anticipate and precipitate the return of Jesus in power, the final manifestation of Elijah. When Jesus returns, He does so with the Sword of the Spirit, which is the Word of God, coming out of His mouth as a sword of fire, a flaming sword. "*Now out of His mouth goes a sharp sword, that with it He should strike the nations*" (Revelation 19:15). When He comes, our ministry in the power and Spirit of Elijah will bring in the kingdom of God on earth, which Jesus will establish in righteousness. As Elijah brought revival to Israel, and

John the Baptist prepared Israel for the New Testament age, so we are being used of God to restore all things ready for His coming.

Even so come, Lord Jesus.

7

THE LATTER RAIN

As rain is poured out in the spring to help germination of the seed, so also does God pour out a harvest rain to bring the crop to a final harvest. These rains are described as former and latter rains in the Bible. Both are necessary for the successful harvest, and as we are now in the harvest time of this age, it is to be expected that we should be in the time of latter rain to swell the grain and prepare it for the great harvest when the angels shall gather it into God's barns. This is why we are instructed by God through His prophet Zechariah to ask for rain in the time of latter rain (see Zechariah 10:1), and this prayer was necessary because there was a great harvest of souls in his day which came about by the spoken Word in the prophecies of both Haggai and Zechariah. In fact, the temple would not have been rebuilt without their prophecies, because the latter rain was sent to confirm God's inheritance when it was weary. (See Psalm 68:9.) They did not just come to preach, but to speak as the oracles of God and give God's children encouragement, exhortation, counsel, and comfort, so that they went right through all the Satanic opposition and built the temple again.

As the true temple was rebuilt in the day of Ezra and Nehemiah, with Haggai and Zechariah prophesying the Word of God, so today, the Elijah ministry with the prophetical Word is being sent again to confirm His weary church, to refresh it, to set it on fire with a renewed outpouring of the Logos. This temple is not built with wood and stone, but with living stones, not made with hands, and this temple composed of Holy Spirit filled men and women, utterly dedicated to the task on hand, will be for the habitation of God through the Spirit. (See Ephesians 2:20–21.)

It is to be regretted that in past times, when there has been a renewed outpouring of the Spirit, instead of this power being canalized and harnessed to bring forth the Word of God, it has frequently degenerated into fleshly excitement and emotion, and so the whole purpose for which the outpouring was sent was lost. It is obvious that when the weary church is refreshed (see Psalm 68:9) it will feel good, but the feelings are not the primary purpose; it is rather that the vessels shall bring forth gifts and fruits in the power of the Spirit.

In Deuteronomy 32, the real purpose of the latter rain is made clear:

> Give ear, O heavens, and **I will speak; and** hear, O earth, **the words of my mouth.** Let my **teaching** drop as the rain, my **speech** distill as the dew, as raindrops on the tender herb, and as showers on the grass. (verses 1–2)

There comes a time when God wishes once again to speak. Most of the time the church has been doing all the speaking, and much that it spoke was inconsequential, without power or authority and its doctrines have so often been wrong, or at least limited. Truly, as Israel of old, the New Testament Israel has limited God. (See Psalm 78:41.) The shameless divisions in Christendom caused by man's ignorance of his Maker and Savior, as well as the lack of the Holy Spirit in the lives of both clergy and congregations, has created a church that is unaware of the voice of God. But this condition is now changing. God is causing His voice to be heard through the charismatic gifts to refresh the members, and to enable them to bring forth the harvest, that this great church—the body of Christ—shall be full of the Word of God.

To most people, doctrine is a boring subject to be avoided. Bible study is the least well attended service of the church, and in many churches there is no Bible study at all, and in others even the morning and evening lessons are not read. The Word of God, which teaches us sound doctrine, is hardly used in the services of some denominations, and so the people are in complete ignorance of the wonderful doctrines that set us free. The very churches hold their flocks in bondage and darkness as bad almost as if they lived without Christ.

The Word of God is coming again to set the people free.

GOD IS CAUSING HIS VOICE TO BE HEARD THROUGH THE CHARISMATIC GIFTS TO REFRESH THE MEMBERS, AND TO ENABLE THEM TO BRING FORTH THE HARVEST, THAT THIS GREAT CHURCH—THE BODY OF CHRIST— SHALL BE FULL OF THE WORD OF GOD.

Possibly the greatest result of this folly is that Satan, knowing that his time is short, is going around with false cults to confuse and interfere with God's true revival (see Revelation 12:12). It has been truly said that, together with God's true revival, Satan is having his revival too, and his revival is based on false doctrine with false prophets at work. God's revival is centered on true doctrine, with true prophets. *"Now I urge you, brethren, note those who cause divisions and offenses, contrary* to the **doctrine** *which you learned, and avoid them*" (Romans 16:17). "If anyone comes to you and does not bring this **doctrine** [the doctrine of Christ], *do not receive him into your house*" (2 John 1:10). Due to the great ignorance of the Word of God with Christians of most denominations, these false prophets have gained entrance not only into houses, but into churches and split them. With the renewed outpouring of the latter rain, the Holy Spirit baptized Christians will be filled with the *Logos* of God. A great hunger will arise, and is arising, for the Word of God. In our service in Toronto, Canada, the Bible study night is now one of the most popular, when every doctrine of Scripture is carefully examined and taught to Holy Spirit filled children of God. When God's inheritance ceases to be weary, they become hungry and keen, and therefore easy to teach, and they in turn easily assimilate the Word into their beings.

In Hosea, there is a remarkable prophecy about this latter rain,

Come and let us return unto the Lord; *for He has torn, but He will heal us; He has stricken, but He will bind us up. After* **two days** *He will* **revive us**; *on the* **third day** *He will raise us up, that* **we may live** *in His sight. Let us know, let us pursue the knowledge of the* Lord. *His going forth is established as the morning; He will come to us like the rain, like the* **latter and former rain** *to the earth.*

(Hosea 6:1–3)

Reckoning on the basis of one day for a thousand years (see 2 Peter 3:8), and beginning at the dates when Israel was cast off for her rebellion between 740–720 BC, and given a bill of divorcement (see Isaiah 50:1), and coming through to the third day, we are brought to AD 1517, which commenced the Protestant revival under Martin Luther, a beginning and a partial reformation of the church; and then we come through the evangelical awakenings of the eighteenth century with the Wesleys, and into the twentieth century with the outpouring of the Spirit in Pentecostal fullness, which brought back the supernatural *Logos* to the church, but much had to be learned. With the renewed outpouring upon all the churches in 1961, we are now witnessing the final stages of the reformation, which will bring a remnant into the fullness of the Spirit and finally unify the church without spot or wrinkle. Thus will the prayer of Jesus be answered, "that we all may be one." (See John 17:21.) This will not be a work of ecumenical councils, but entirely a work of the Spirit, as He is outpoured as the former and latter rain. The whole of the outpouring occurs within the period of the third day of Hosea's prophecy, and let us note the things that occur.

God will heal us. This means complete healing for spirit, soul and body—a return of divine healing. He will bind us up; divine love and compassion comes with the return of the Holy Spirit's outpouring. The story of the Good Samaritan has an echo of this. In the *third day*, or the period covered by the Reformation (1517 to the end), He will raise us up and we shall live in His sight. As the manna came down each day from heaven like dew and soft rain, so also does the manna—the bread of life (see John 6:51)—come down from heaven in the form of the life-giving latter rain. During the time that Israel fed on manna, they had no single sick or feeble persons among their tribes (see Psalm 105:37), because the manna was such a perfect food. It sustained them in perfect health. The Word of God—the *Logos*—is our perfect food, and as we allow ourselves to receive the refreshing of the latter rain today, and take down the umbrellas of our traditions and unbelief, we shall find that God will begin healing us, binding us up, and causing us to live in perfect health. Amazing but true! What a far cry from our traditional forms of Christianity, but this is the end result of the present outpouring of the Holy Spirit.

In the wonderful second chapter of Joel, wherein he tells us that "*the Lord gives voice before His army; for His camp is very great*" (verse 11), he goes on and enlarges the vision and tells New Testament Zion to "*rejoice in the Lord your God; for He has given you the former rain faithfully, and He will cause the rain to come down for you—the former rain, and the latter rain in the first month*" (verse 23). As the former rain came moderately on the day of Pentecost to create the body of Christ, so in exactly the same manner, will the latter rain come as at first (the word "*month*" is not in the original), without moderation. It is prophesied to be on all flesh (see verses 28–29) and *"to the end of the earth"* (Acts 1:8). As Elijah saw the cloud the size of a man's hand, which he interpreted as a token of the deluge to come, he started to outrun the chariot of wicked Ahab, for it is written: *"It happened in the meantime that the sky became black with clouds and wind, and there was a heavy rain"* (1 Kings 18:45).

The sign of the coming of the Holy Spirit on the day of Pentecost was a rushing wind, and the heavens discharged the latter rain moderately, and the first 120 members of the body of Christ started speaking in other languages as the Holy Spirit gave them the Words. The *Logos* had returned in the power of the Spirit. It is always a source of great blessing to read that Mary the mother of Jesus was among the charter members. This should encourage our Catholic friends, who are now receiving the Holy Spirit. The Holy Spirit is becoming a person to many instead of a doctrine!

We cannot end this chapter on the latter rain without reference to the writings of the apostle James.

> *Be patient, brethren, until the coming of the Lord. See how the farmer waits for the precious fruit of the earth, waiting patiently for it until it receives the **early and latter rain**…. For the coming of the Lord is at hand.* (James 5:7–8)

The greatest sign of the near return of Jesus Christ to this earth to fulfill the many prophecies (see Acts 1:11) is the coming of the Holy Spirit to reveal Jesus in His body the church before His literal descent with clouds (see Revelation 1:7). The latter rain is preparing the precious fruit for the return of Christ. The gifts of the Spirit, when used through oracles of God, are continually reminding us of the return of Jesus to this earth to rule and reign over His kingdom in equity and justice. (See Isaiah 9:6–7.) It is an amazing fact that as soon as a person receives the wonderful baptism of the Spirit and speaks in tongues, the result is that they get right back to the Bible and the Holy Spirit begins to teach them! Thus we can look forward to the time when the counsel of Paul will be realized, *"Now I plead with you, brethren, by the name of our Lord Jesus Christ, that you all **speak the same thing**, and that there be no divisions among you, but that you be perfectly joined together in the same mind"* (1 Corinthians 1:10). Only the baptism in the Spirit can accomplish such a miracle, and this miracle is taking place today. If we have all received the same Word, we must all speak the same thing. Do you see?

*"Ask the L*ORD *for rain in the time of the **latter rain**"* (Zechariah 10:1). This is the time to pray for the heavens to become black with clouds, and for there to be a cloudburst upon us all. Amen.

8

THE BODY OF CHRIST

It is generally accepted that an individual is made a member of Christ by the rebirth at conversion, but we must remember that Jesus, although He became the Word made flesh at His birth (see John 1:14), when an earthly body was created for Him in which He was to dwell among us, He did not commence to manifest the power of God in His body until He received the anointing of the Holy Spirit at the age of thirty. Apart from one reference to His astonishing knowledge when He was twelve, no further reference is made of His supernatural abilities until He became the Anointed One (in Greek, *Christos*) by the coming of the Holy Spirit following His obedience in water baptism. (See Daniel 9:24.) It was after this anointing that He returned in the *power* of the Spirit (see Luke 4:14) and entered in synagogues, and cast out demons, and healed the sick. It was after this anointing that the people said "*Never man spake like this man*" (John 7:46), and it is recorded that they were astonished at His doctrine, for His Word was with *power*.

The apostle Paul wrote to us today in this twentieth century:

> *...having been built on the foundation of the apostles and prophets, Jesus Christ Himself being the chief cornerstone, in whom the whole building, being fitted together, grows into a* **holy temple** *in the Lord, in whom you also are being built together for a dwelling place of God in the Spirit.* (Ephesians 2:20–22)

It is clear that we become living, or lively stones, framed together by the Holy Spirit in the body of Christ which is *"a dwelling place of God."* It is the temple of God. It is that through which God wishes to manifest Himself, and none other. In 1 Corinthians 12:7, the *charismata* are referred to as manifestations of the Spirit. These nine manifestations of tongues, interpretation of tongues, prophecy, faith, gifts of healing, working of miracles, discerning of spirits, the word of knowledge and wisdom, are *manifestations* of the chief Cornerstone, who said He, and He alone, would build this church—*His own body.*

The church, which is built on the ministry of the apostles and prophets, is not an organization, it is not a denomination, it is not a society, it is not a collection of disciples (there were disciples before Pentecost). It is built of willing men and women, utterly dedicated to the task of revealing Jesus, and this can only be done by the Spirit of God, dwelling in each member who thereby become fitly framed together.

As we look at our powerful denominations, our theological colleges and seminaries, our Christian organizations, we see man determining what he is going to do for God, rather than to allow himself to be a channel through whom God may manifest Himself in the person of the Logos through our flesh—His body! God has today prepared a body for His Son, even as He did for His Son when He ministered on earth. Satan caused the crucifixion of that body—that Holy Spirit anointed body—but God brought good out of evil and Satan was defeated by this act, and now the body has become so enlarged that it covers the whole earth and there are Holy Spirit filled members in every country of the world. Each assembly of these Holy Spirit anointed saints should manifest Jesus in the power of His Spirit, through the nine manifestations already referred to. Jesus said of His disciples *before* Pentecost that they had their names written in heaven (see Luke 10:21), and the sick were manifestly healed and demons cast out *before* Pentecost. Why then bother to bring these men and women to a personal Pentecost with the "embarrassment" of tongues? Why not leave them in their own groups rejoicing in their salvation and healing? God wanted to use them, as one body—anointed and charged to overflowing with the Holy Spirit— so that His Word could be manifest through them corporately in the power of the Spirit; the Word that would edify, bless, encourage, comfort, strengthen, heal, deliver, and cast the devil out of lives. The body of Christ was to be a vehicle of the flowing Word of God. This is why He said that rivers would flow out of their innermost parts—but not before the baptism in the Spirit was experienced by each individual stone, fitly framing them together as one composite temple—the body of Christ with Jesus as the chief cornerstone. He determines the angles of the building, and our angles must be His angles.

THE BODY OF CHRIST WAS TO BE A VEHICLE OF THE FLOWING WORD OF GOD. THIS IS WHY HE SAID THAT RIVERS WOULD FLOW OUT OF THEIR INNERMOST PARTS.

Members of this temple do not carry a denominational tag. They are filled with Father, Son, and Holy Spirit, and this is what was meant by Jesus in John 14:20, when He referred to the outpouring of the Holy Spirit on the day of Pentecost in these words, *"At that day you will **know** that I am in My Father, and you in Me, and I in you."* Up to this time, they were unable even to comprehend that Jesus was in His Father, and that His Father was in Jesus. (See John 14:10–11.) In their unanointed carnality, they could not understand how God could actually indwell His

Son, and how the Son could indwell the Father. This was a mystery far too deep for the finite mind of man, and Jesus knew this and told them that on the Day of Pentecost they would know and understand. It was necessary for them to be baptized in the Spirit. It takes the indwelling of the Third Person in baptizing power to give us supernatural understanding of the mysteries of God. This is why so much theology makes no sense to the Holy Spirit, because it comes from the wisdom of man, which God tells us is foolishness with Him. (See 1 Corinthians 2:14.)

Many ministers have testified that after Jesus baptized them in the Holy Spirit, they realized how much nonsense bad been taught them by the mind of men. Before their personal Pentecost, they taught man-made doctrines from their minds, but after their Pentecost they became channels for the flow of the supernatural Word of God in wisdom and understanding. Truly, it is the same today, *"At that day you will know"* (John 14:20). You must come to that day—your personal day of Pentecost. If you do not, you will not be able to understand the purposes of God in creating the church which is the body of Christ.

If Jesus did not attempt to manifest the power of God before He was anointed to begin the work of the Christ, how much more we, who claim to be members of Christ, should not attempt to minister, either as laymen, or ordained ministers, until we have been anointed with that anointing which Jesus called the baptism in the Spirit. He baptizes us into the Holy Spirit, and then we overflow with supernatural manifestations of the Holy Spirit, beginning with tongues! This initial manifestation is only the beginning of the outflow of the *Logos*—the Word of God.

We were talking to a minister of the Southern Baptist denomination who received his personal Pentecost while praying in his study, because he was dissatisfied with programs, committees, people, carnality, and entertainment in the church. These did not satisfy. No one had told him about a personal Pentecost—he had avoided those who claimed to speak in tongues, believing them to belong to the fanatical fringe of the church. He knew nothing about the baptism in the Spirit doctrinally—why should he? No one had ever taught him about in seminary.

God met his earnest cry to heaven for power to minister as he believed they did in the early church. Suddenly, and without outward emotion, he began to speak words of another language. His whole being was supernaturally charged—he had never had an experience like this before; something unusual had happened! He went into his home and met his wife, who saw his face was aglow with a divine radiance. She knelt with him and soon she also was manifesting glossolalia. This faithful pastor began to minister in the power of the Spirit. Others in the church also received their personal Pentecost, including his deacons. People were healed, programs disappeared, head-counting stopped. Some people left, but more came, because the gifts of the Spirit, the manifestations of the *Logos* began to appear. The deacons of the church were filled to overflowing, and now this same denominational church has become a New Testament Assembly to manifest Jesus, the Word of Life! No more straining in the energy of the flesh to do God's work man's way—now just resting in the Lord and permitting God by the Spirit to manifest Jesus in their midst! What a contrast! What a blessing!

This church—the body of Christ—is God's secret weapon which will yet upset the counsels of man whether in government or church. Let Satan have his servants and schemers, but God has His Spirit, which He is now pouring out upon His church. This is not a denominational organization, it is composed of men and women of every race, all baptized in one Spirit in one body. Incidentally, this is the literal meaning of 1 Corinthians 12:13, all have been made to drink *into* one Spirit.

In this present outpouring of the Spirit upon the church, as promised in the Word of God, denominational walls come crumbling down, for this glorious baptism in the Spirit truly makes them all one in Christ, as never before. If He, in His great power, could do nothing unless the Father did it through Him, how much more we, members of His body, not try to be anything or do anything without the baptism in the Spirit to manifest Jesus in and through us!

One of the purposes of this book is to teach those who have already received this glorious personal Pentecost why they did receive, for many are worshipping in churches where the gifts or manifestations of the

Spirit are never heard. They worship in man-made program churches. Surely this must quench the power of the Word resident in them by the indwelling Spirit! If you cannot find a true New Testament church in your area in which all nine gifts are regularly manifest, then gather in groups with those of like mind and experience, and ask Jesus to manifest Himself through you in times of prayer. This will bring new meaning to His Word, "*Where two or three are gathered together in My name, I am there in the midst of them*" (Matthew 18:20). Pray also that God will supply the necessary anointed oversight. Thus will New Testament Spirit-filled Christians be edified, and be able to teach and encourage others in our churches for this glorious end-time visitation of the Spirit of God upon hungry lives. Do not disassociate yourself from a local church completely, but help it.

THIS REVIVAL OR CHARISMATIC RENEWAL HAS ONLY BEGUN. IT WILL SWEEP THROUGH LIKE A DELUGE, BREAKING DOWN MAN-MADE BARRIERS OF SPIRITUAL EXPRESSION, AND PRODUCE A CHURCH—HIS BODY—THAT WILL BE SO INVINCIBLE IN A COMPROMISING WORLD THAT SATAN WILL TREMBLE AND HAVE TO ACKNOWLEDGE HIS DEFEAT AT CALVARY.

This revival or charismatic renewal has only begun. It will sweep through like a deluge, breaking down man-made barriers of spiritual expression, and produce a church—His body—that will be so invincible in a compromising world that Satan will tremble and have to acknowledge his defeat at Calvary. Jesus said of His church that the gates of hell would not prevail against it. Sin, sickness, error, carnality, and demons will be swept away before the mighty torrent of living waters flowing out of the innermost parts of millions of living stones, fitly framed together by the Holy Spirit. As Jesus, the *Stone*, was smitten at Calvary, and living waters flowed out of Him at Pentecost, so today, we, as stones made after the likeness of *the* Stone, will find waters gushing out of ourselves in desert places, because the Headstone was smitten of God! The miracle of waters gushing out of the smitten stone in the desert will be repeated in millions of stones today, for the same purpose, to *"make a road in the wilderness, and rivers in the desert"* (Isaiah 43:19) so that His people may drink. This is called "doing a new thing"!

The disorganized churches and the over-organized churches will be given an opportunity to come and drink at the fountain of waters in the desert of ecclesiasticism, sacerdotalism (belief that sin sacrifices require the intervention of a priest), and entertainment.

The *living Word—the Christ*—has come down to deliver.

PULLING DOWN STRONGHOLDS

CONTENTS

INTRODUCTION

Pulling Down Strongholds is a book that every present-day Christian should read.

Too long have the churches of our Lord and Savior Jesus Christ preached an almost powerless gospel. Much of today's teaching and preaching in our churches of the twentieth century is so lacking in the fundamental biblical truths, that one is prone to wonder how people can trust Jesus Christ with the mighty matter of their eternal salvation when they have not as yet been taught to trust Him in the everyday affairs of this present life.

The Bible promises us, *"My God shall supply all your need according to His riches in glory by Christ Jesus"* (Philippians 4:19). Yet, all about us, we see defeated, discouraged, ailing, and needy Christians. It is tragic to see God's people so completely fettered by Satan and his demons. Safe to say, the Lord God never intended for His people to live in such bondage and subjection.

Jesus declared, "*And you shall know the truth, and the truth shall make you free.*" (John 8:32). *Pulling Down Strongholds*, a book replete with scriptural truth, will be an eye opener to any believing Christian who is willing to lay aside old misconceptions and to permit the Lord to speak to his heart concerning our true heritage in Jesus Christ.

When one considers that the prophecies of the Bible are largely fulfilled, and that, therefore, we are living in the last days, be this period longer or shorter than we might suppose, one begins to ask himself what else must be accomplished before our Lord returns? The answer to this question seems obvious to me. The church, that body of true believers, must take her rightful place in God's plan. The Lord Jesus Christ awaits our awakening from the sleep of spiritual lethargy. How the heart of God must agonize over our failure to utilize what He has purchased for us in Christ's own precious blood.

The Word of our Lord calls to us through His servant Paul:

"*Awake, you who sleep, arise from the dead, and Christ will give you light.*" *See then that you walk circumspectly, not as fools but as wise, redeeming the time, because the days are evil. Therefore do not be unwise, but understand what the will of the Lord is. And do not be drunk with wine, in which is dissipation; but be filled with the Spirit.* (Ephesians 5:14–18)

For said Jesus, "*You shall receive power when the Holy Spirit has come upon you*" (Acts 1:8). Personally, I must agree with Brother Whyte; I believe that this power is even unto *Pulling Down Strongholds*.

—*Pastor Frank A. Downing*
Baltimore, Maryland
February 1964

1

WHAT IS MAN?

In Psalm 8:4, we find this pertinent question, "*What is man?*" Surely we see him as the most contradictory, irrational, irresponsible creature in God's universe. He does things that animals would not do; he feeds on things animals would ignore; he lies, he cheats, he steals, and he kills. He is capable of creating great masterpieces of music and art; he can find medicines to heal himself, and at the same time, invent means of destroying himself. Try as one might, it is difficult to see anything that makes very much sense about so-called "Homo Sapiens."

Did God create man that he should behave like this? It may be supposed that his incredible behavior is a reason why some do not believe that God made him, for would God make anything so vile? And yet, he is capable of such rich and fine things.

The apostle Paul gave us an answer. He was not impressed with man and he wrote a most unpleasant story about him; he painted a picture that is repulsive, knowing that the prophet Jeremiah had said long before that man's heart was desperately wicked, so wicked that he is unable to understand why he acts as he does.

Paul wrote that there was not one righteous man. Did he exaggerate? As we look around our big cities, in our businesses, our factories, and our farms, is there not one righteous man? "No, not one" is the verdict of the Holy Bible. No wonder it makes unpopular reading! Here is a list of the shortcomings of man as Paul saw him:

- None understands.
- None seeks God.
- All have gone out of the way.
- All are unprofitable.
- None does good.
- Their throats are open sepulchers.
- They use their tongues for deceit.
- Under their lips is the poison of asps.
- They curse with bitterness.
- They shed blood.
- They destroy and are miserable.
- They know no peace.
- They do not fear God.

These thirteen condemnatory characteristics describe mankind without God in his thoughts. This is the natural man in our streets and cities. Man without God—the unbeliever. He may go to church, he may be agnostic, and he may even say he is atheistic, but these thirteen points describe him perfectly.

"What is man?" asked the psalmist. "A strange creature indeed," we would reply.

Did God create man to behave in this irresponsible and illogical way? Was man as we see him today the pattern of mankind that God created? No, a thousand times no—man is far removed from the picture that God had (and has) in mind when He created him. Something must have happened between the creation of man and the present-day caricature. This happening was the fall of man from his high estate in the garden of Eden.

In Psalm 8, David explained what God had in mind in the beginning. Even now, God is still mindful of man; that is to say, God cares and God loves him, even if he is a fallen creature, and did indeed visit him in the Person of the Lord Jesus Christ.

In verse 5, we read that God created man a little lower than the angels; not a great deal lower, but "a little lower." Before He created mankind, God created the angelic realm of thousands upon thousands of glorious spiritual beings, who are called angels or messengers of God. They are wonderful and powerful, but even among this great creation, one-third fell also from their first high estate and were cast into the earth as "fallen angels"; and as they fell with Satan, they became his angels, or messengers. We read, *"So the great dragon was cast out, that serpent of old, called the Devil and Satan, who deceives the whole world; he was cast to the earth, and his angels were cast out with him"* (Revelation 12:9). Man would have remained the wonderful creation that he was in Eden if Satan and his angels had not preceded him there. Satan tempted Adam and Eve and they both fell, and in turn, they also were cast out of Eden, the earthly paradise.

IN THE BEGINNING, MAN WAS CREATED TO HAVE *DOMINION* OVER ALL THE WORKS OF GOD'S HANDS. NOTHING ON THIS EARTH WAS TO HAVE DOMINION OVER MAN. MAN WAS TO BE STRONGER THAN CIRCUMSTANCES. MAN WAS MADE TO GO OVER, NOT GO UNDER.

God cannot have either sin or sinners in His presence, either in heaven or on earth. Fallen man cannot dwell in the presence of God. It is only as God visited man in the person of Jesus Christ that the way back to His presence, His glory, His blessings, and His kingdom was made. Although man was cast out of Eden, a way is made for him to return and recapture all his past glory (and more). Jesus, *"I am the way, the truth, and the life"* (John 14:6).

In the beginning, man was created to have *dominion* over all the works of God's hands. Nothing on this earth was to have dominion over man. Man was to be stronger than circumstances. Man was made to go over, not go under. He was to have dominion over all animals; sheep and powerful oxen, lions and tigers, rhinoceros and elephants, rats and mice—germs! He was to have the rule over everything that flies, including the eagle; no fish was to be too great for him, even whales would be subject to him. The trees and vegetation, the minerals would all be ruled over by God's man—not Satan's man! It is Satan's fear that causes man not to believe this and run from beasts. *"For you did not receive the spirit of bondage again to fear, but you received the Spirit"* (Romans 8:15). God does not intend man to be afraid of anybody or anything!

In Genesis 1, we have the sacred record of man's creation. *"So God created man **in His own image**; in the image of God He created him; male and female He created them"* (verse 27). This man, having God's image and likeness, was to multiply himself on the earth with similar sons of God, made in God's likeness. God's original purpose (which has not changed) was that this earth was to be filled with men and women created in the image of God. God-men and God-women all over this planet. What a paradise—and it will yet be so; God's purpose will triumph in the end, and this world will yet be filled with the glory of God. God has made a way, mankind must enter into that way, and he will become a son of God, a God-man again, with all his previous dominion given back *in Christ.*

The earth was to be replenished by these lovely God-men and God-women, not the vain strutting fashion models, or conceited educated man, but by humble, powerful, gracious humans; and they were to subdue the world and have it under their control, not under any other power. God-men were to rule the world, not dictators or imperialists. No fear, no wars, no famines, no want, but plenty for everyone. This was God's original intention, and He has not forsaken His throne or His purposes for puny rebellious man. *"He who sits in the heavens shall laugh; the Lord shall hold them in derision"* (Psalm 2:4).

God's men were to have *dominion* over animals, fishes, and birds. Nothing that moves on the earth was to have dominion over man. (See Genesis 1:26–28.)

So when David asked that question, "What is man?" in Psalm 8, he was looking at God's promises, and not at the travesty that walks our streets today. Even so, we should always see, or try to see, as God sees things, by believing His Word and all His wonderful promises. As we continue in this little study of man's authority in Christ, we shall marvel that such provision has already been made for sinful man to rise higher even than the angelic realm, *on earth*. Let us look through the window of God's Word and not at the changing circumstances all around us. Man will let you down, but Jesus will lift you up!

2

JESUS—THE WAY UP

Jesus told us that *"I am the way, the truth, and the life"* (John 14:6). In this triad, we have the recipe for a life of dominion over the world, the flesh, and the devil. There is not a created being, be it an elephant or a germ, that can harm a son of God, *unless we permit it to harm us by fear!* Once we have fully understood our authority vested in us by God through Christ, we can progressively and experimentally take our place as invincible creatures of faith, and not conquerable captives of fear. Paul wrote, *"We are more than conquerors through [Christ]"* (Romans 8:37). Not just conquerors, but *more than* conquerors. When Satan and his cohorts view us in this light, it is not surprising that the Bible teaches that *"the wicked one does not touch him"* (1 John 5:18)!

Jesus is *the way* out of our captivity, our bondage, our sorrows, and our feebleness. He blazed a trail clean out of captivity. He was manifest and anointed with the Holy Spirit at Jordan, that He might bind up the brokenhearted, proclaim liberty to the captives, open the prison doors to those who were bound in chains, and to set them free. This fullness of salvation is not necessary to be repeated. We are saved, and set free once and for all, that we might enjoy a fullness of blessing in this kingdom of God on earth—restored Paradise indeed. The salvation of the soul is the way into the new life, with healing of the mind and body, so that we might enjoy divine health and strength. The prison door is not opened that we might come out one day and go back in a week's time because we got so used to "being cared for by the devil." It was said that many slaves who were emancipated in the days of Abraham Lincoln continued to work for their old masters, rather than venture forth into an unknown world. Truly, the kingdom of God is an unknown world to most people, and unfortunately so few Christians today have much idea of the blessing given by Jesus to us on the cross. They would rather live like other church-going people, than begin to act as sons of God—royalty indeed. Being of the royal family of God sets them too far apart from even members of their own families, who remain in sin and ignorance. They dare not be different. However, the Bible teaches us that we are different—completely different and separate from the world. It is as we learn to live and act differently that we begin to have experiences of divine power, authority, and blessing that amaze us, and demonstrate God's glory.

Jesus said, "I am...the **truth**." Once we have accepted the way, we must walk in the light as He is in the light. (See 1 John 1:7.) We no longer walk by traditions taught to us by others, even if these traditions sounded so sensible, and were taught by church leaders. In Jesus's day, there were many rabbis, and a powerful church, but He said they had made the Word of God of none effect by their traditions. This means, in plain language, they had thrown the Book out of the window. They had church, ceremonies, religion, priests, and services, but *no truth*. Once a son of God enters the kingdom of God, he must adjust his life, his thinking, his speech, and his bearing, and realize that *"perfect love casts out fear"* (1 John 4:18). What a challenge. The more our lives become readjusted to His truth, the more authority we will exercise over Satan. Though all men may laugh at you, it is better to obey God than man.

Jesus said, "I am...the **life**." Christianity is not an imitation of the life of Christ (even if that were possible). It is not obeying "your church."

It is not a monastic life suppressing natural desires and appetites. It is a life of abundance for spirit, soul, and body. Jesus said that He came to give *life* and to give it more abundantly. He came to take that tired, bound, captive life and fill it with His overwhelming abundance. (See John 10:10.) Can we imagine Adam being sick, depressed, miserable, weak, and fearful in the garden? Jesus came to give us back everything that Adam lost, and, as we shall see, even more under the new covenant in His blood. *Abundant life* means just what it says for every child of God, everyone who approaches the mercy seat will have made available immediately every blessing in the Bible, and there are thousands. Abundant life, including joy, peace, strength, health, and prosperity, is laid to your account in heaven by Jesus Christ. *"My God shall supply all your need according to His riches in glory by Christ Jesus"* (Philippians 4:19). Unfortunately, when a child of God does venture into the bank of heaven, after knocking timorously, instead of walking in boldly as if he owned the place (and he does!), he usually cautiously and apologetically approaches one of the tellers, and proffers a check with a small amount and frankly wonders whether it will be honored! This is not an exaggeration concerning the approach in prayer of the average child of God. We might just as well write "million" as "two," because it belongs to an heir of God anyway. Let us therefore go *boldly* into the holiest place by a new and living way, and plead the blood of Jesus as our reason for expecting fantastic blessings. The world uses the word "pay off." Our "pay off" includes everything the moment we dare to enjoy it by faith. The blood of Jesus purchased every redemptive blessing for us.

"But I am not worthy of His blessings." Who said so? The opposite is the truth; this is a lie of Satan. *"You have a few names...who have not defiled their garments; and they shall walk with Me in white, **for they are worthy**"* (Revelation 3:4). Jesus makes us worthy in Him. As long as we abide in Him, and permit His Words to abide in us, then we will continue to walk worthy of all His abundant blessings. Though these wonderful blessings have been made available to us at the cross, yet each promise must be appropriated by our own personal faith, and not that of another; no promise of God is automatically bestowed on us. It must be appropriated by faith.

The story is told of a soldier son who faithfully sent his uneducated mother a monthly check, enough to keep her in comfort, health, and happiness. The mother could not read, and so she received her son's letters, but she did not understand what the check was, and so, over a period of years, she stuffed the checks into her mattress. She died in abject poverty, bringing early death upon herself because of lack of proper food. Had she not the means? Were not the checks good? Was not the son faithful in all that he did? Had she understood the ways of the bank and of her son, she need not have died in misery. She was worthy for she was his mother. We are worthy of these blessings because we are sons. Ignorance is robbing Christians of their blessings, because we do not know our throne rights. This book is helping to expose the cruel bondage of Satan, and to open the windows of heaven that such a blessing will be poured out that we shall not be able to contain! (See Malachi 3:10.)

ABUNDANT LIFE MEANS JUST WHAT IT SAYS FOR EVERY CHILD OF GOD, EVERYONE WHO APPROACHES THE MERCY SEAT WILL HAVE MADE AVAILABLE IMMEDIATELY EVERY BLESSING IN THE BIBLE, AND THERE ARE THOUSANDS. ABUNDANT LIFE, INCLUDING JOY, PEACE, STRENGTH, HEALTH, AND PROSPERITY, IS LAID TO YOUR ACCOUNT IN HEAVEN BY JESUS CHRIST.

You must walk in the *way*; you must feed upon His *truth*; and you must live the more abundant *life*. God will not make us do anything. He offers, we receive, and we use. Jesus did His part on Calvary, and it was perfectly done. There is nothing for us to do except gratefully take and use.

3

A KINGDOM OF POWER

Jesus said, "*If I cast out demons with the finger of God, surely the kingdom of God has come upon you*" (Luke 11:20). The proof of the restored kingdom of God among men was the tremendous demonstration of the power of God over every other power. This power and authority becomes ours as we enter into this kingdom by faith in Jesus as Savior. Not only are we saved from the power and penalty of sin, but we are delivered to a position of authority whereby we can now exercise God's divine power over all other powers, secular, ecclesiastical, or demonic. Jesus ushered in a new dispensation which was so vastly different from that exercised by the priesthood that they failed to see His kingdom at all. Are there not many in our churches like this today?

"*No man ever spoke like this Man!*" (John 7:46). "*He taught them as one having authority, and not as the scribes*" (Matthew 7:29). "*Even the winds and the sea obey Him*" (Matthew 8:27). These were some of the many statements made by those who saw Him minister. They were both astonished and offended. He put them to silence by deeds, not words;

*"for the kingdom of God is not in word **but in power**"* (1 Corinthians 4:20). *"The works that I do he will do also; and greater works than these he will do"* (John 14:12). Those who accept the Son and believe on Him are given His authority and His ability to work the works of Jesus right here on earth. This is the plain meaning of the words of Jesus, and no amount of apologetics or reasoning will reduce the plain meaning of Scripture. If it is believed and acted upon, the Words become alive, and bring forth results; if they are rejected and not believed, then we continue in our unbelief and misery, even if we claim to be sons of God. James said, *"Thus also faith by itself, if it does not have works, is dead.... I will show you my faith by my works"* (James 2:17–18).

Jesus came first to demonstrate this new kingdom. He then chose twelve others unto whom He gave His authority, and He sent them out to preach that the kingdom of God had arrived, and they were told they had His power and authority to cast out *all demons* and to cure all diseases. (See Luke 9:12). Among these men were fishermen, a tax gatherer, and a medical doctor. They were not required to bring their skills, they were only required to use His authority, and then to expect things to begin to happen. Many have supposed the first twelve apostles were super men. They were in one sense, but first, they became humble men to do supernatural miracles of healing. Natural man doing supernatural things. Is this possible for us today? Certainly. Jesus has not changed, neither has His kingdom.

Thank God, this wonderful miracle working ability did not stop with the apostles, neither was it confined to them. God wants us all to exercise this authority today, both men and women, and to do the signs and wonders and miracles that He did when on earth, for today He is on earth in us, members of His body.

It is recorded of these twelve that they departed and were obedient and went into the towns, preaching the gospel and healing *everywhere!* (See Luke 9:6.) No limited gospel here; no system of apologetics; no explanation for failures; and let us note well that this occurred before the cross and before the New Testament Church was born on the day of Pentecost. The cross was the dividing line between the Old and New

Testaments, so if these miracles were done on the Old Testament side of the cross, how much more should we be doing these things on the New Testament side? What a challenge we have, to preach and work the works of Jesus.

GOD WANTS US ALL TO EXERCISE THIS AUTHORITY TODAY, BOTH MEN AND WOMEN, AND TO DO THE SIGNS AND WONDERS AND MIRACLES THAT HE DID WHEN ON EARTH, FOR TODAY HE IS ON EARTH IN US, MEMBERS OF HIS BODY.

Jesus was the firstfruit of a new creation. There quickly followed twelve apostles, who were equally quickly followed by seventy ordinary men. These seventy might have had a lesser rank, but they certainly did not have less power or authority! We are not to suppose that they were specially educated for this ministry, or that they were more than a cross section of society of their day. It is not known whether there were any priests or scribes among them, but there is no suggestion that there were. It is more likely that they were tradesmen, craftsmen, and businessmen. To these additional seventy, Jesus gave the same authority and power as to the apostles, and they also went forth into different towns and villages. It would seem they were unfamiliar with our modern tools of evangelism, and perhaps it is just as well that they were, for we do not get the same results with these tools as they did with His authority!

"Then the seventy returned with joy, saying, 'Lord, even the demons are subject to us in Your name'" (Luke 10:17). Now, how did they know there were any demons? Today in our churches, the word is hardly mentioned,

and our testimony would not be received well if we explained that there were billions of them! Jesus Christ healed all who were oppressed of the devil. (See Acts 10:38.) Satan can only oppress, vex, and torment by his demons, he is not omnipresent! They are his agents. The first missionary journey undertaken by this group of seventy, who went two by two into every town, was to seek out those who were sick, and to tell them the kingdom of God had come unto them. The proof of divine healing was the proof of the kingdom!

In November 1963, I was privileged to preach in a church seating five hundred people in Atlixco, Mexico. It was a martyr church, having lost nine members over the years who had been murdered by religious fanatics. One man heard the truth of the gospel, of how Jesus promised to heal the sick, and so he went home to his town with the love of God and the authority of Jesus. He was a very unlearned man, as the world counts education. He wanted to establish a New Testament church (they had plenty of other types of churches) and so he wondered what he should do to make the first move to preach. He felt led of the Spirit to go to the drug store in Atlixco, and saw a man going into it. He asked him if there was sickness in his home and the man said there was. Our brother then told him he knew of a Physician who would heal him and offered to introduce him. The man made his purchase and gladly took this disciple back to his home, whereupon he explained that Jesus was the Physician and proceeded to pray for the sick people in the home, and Jesus healed them all. He then returned to the drug store and found a woman going inside, and he told her the same things and accompanied her back to her home, prayed for the sick, and Jesus healed them all. This method was used to establish a New Testament assembly just a few years ago. After they grew in numbers, the devil stirred up opposition to them, and they were all cast into prison, and then they found to their joy that Paul and Silas were also cast into prison for the same reason, and so they began singing hymns at the tops of their voices (and these people can sing!), and finally the prison authorities could stand it no longer and released them all. They even carried their faith to surprising limits. A man's horse fell sick, so they realized that a horse was also a creature of

God and was a blessing to the owner, so they got an extra-large bottle of oil (because the horse was large) and poured it all over the large horse in the name of Jesus, and the horse recovered. This story was told to me by the members of the church, who now worship in a large building without opposition.

When the disciples of Jesus returned with joy, he explained to them the reason for their success. May we not hearken well to what He said? *"Behold, I give unto you* **power** *to tread on serpents and scorpions, and over* **all the power** *of the enemy* [Satan]: *and nothing shall by any means hurt you"* (Luke 10:19 KJV). *"Power to tread"*—He was only echoing what the psalmist had said, that which was written on the sacred Jewish scrolls: *"You shall tread upon the lion and the cobra, the young lion and the serpent you shall trample underfoot"* (Psalm 91:13). This was no new doctrine. Jesus was just bringing it up to date, to demonstrate in His dispensation that God is greater than all the works of the devil. Two feet to tread on serpents and scorpions. We do not exaggerate if we suggest that our two feet may be firmly placed upon the sins and the sicknesses that assail us. Moses took the serpent by the tail and it became harmless, and the seed of the woman was to bruise the head of the serpent (see Genesis 3:15), and it is by crushing our foot upon serpents heads that we destroy them. *"Sin shall not have dominion over you"* (Romans 6:14), wrote Paul, because we should have dominion over sin. We must put our feet firmly upon both sin and sickness, the double curse, if we are to live a life of victory every day. It is possible; it is provided for; Jesus's authority is complete, for we are complete in Him. (See Colossians 2:10.)

We also have two hands to hold on to the right hand of God, the holy arm of the Lord (see Psalm 98:1), for it is this holy arm and hand that has gotten us the victory. Hold on tight to Jesus every day, and tread upon Satan every day, and we are safe for time and eternity.

4

HIS AUTHORITY IS FOR US ALL

Some have tried to hide behind the fallacy that Jesus only vested His authority in the twelve apostles. These twelve men were the foundation stones of the New Testament church, and they were built upon Jesus the *cornerstone*. They were the messengers of the new covenant, but the church—the body of Christ—is composed of many members, and these are supposed to exercise His authority each day in their own lives, so that the church shall arrive at a point of having no spot or wrinkle, no sickness nor disease, no defeat nor frustration, and no oppression of Satan. We are told to go on unto perfection!

Before Jesus left this earth, He gave a last commission to His church, which was not a limited dispensational commission, but binding for the whole Christian age or dispensation, which ceases at His second coming, and then we shall be like Him. In Matthew 28:18, Jesus told His disciples that He had been given *all power* in heaven and upon earth. He had earned this power by His death and the shedding of His blood. The whole power of the universe was vested in one Man who rose from the dead. Because of the death of the Testator, the new covenant now came into operation, and as in the case of common earthly testaments, or wills, the Father left all to His Only Son. God in Christ *died*, reconciling the world unto Himself, and in this manner was the new covenant ushered in when Jesus shed His blood and gave up the spirit on the cross, crying *"It is finished!"* (John 19:30). Because God died in the person of Christ, it became legally possible for His Son to possess all things, and because He possessed them, He had a free hand to give them to whomsoever He wished. The gifts and callings of God are without repentance, and Jesus His Son was called to bring in the kingdom of God upon earth, to establish it, to order and govern it. (See Isaiah 9:6–7.)

It was this thought that was no doubt in His mind when He gave seventy men His power, for it was His to give by right of sacrifice. When they dared to us it in faith—it worked! This should not surprise any of us, for we have a demonstration of higher authority every day in the police force of any nation or city. When the policeman holds up his hand in traffic, the vehicles grind to a halt, because the authority of the head of state is vested in that policeman's hand! In the British Commonwealth, that authority belongs to the queen or king, and is known as the authority of The Crown. When we accept Jesus as Savior, we accept the authority of the *crown*, for we are a royal priesthood, we are kings and priests, we are of royal family, we enforce the law of Calvary! His crown covers our authority and when we hold up our hands before all the might of Satan, he also must grind to a complete stop. Can we give Satan a ticket? Certainly, we can give him one with these words, *"Do you not know that we shall judge angels?"* (1 Corinthians 6:3), for the day is coming when God will permit us to rule over His kingdom with Him, and to judge righteous judgment in His name. Even demons and Satan are under God's judgment through us. He knows it, but he tries to keep the truth from us and keep us in ignorance, so that we do not exercise this tremendous power. Satan is a defeated foe.

Therefore, it is in keeping with the gospel that we should all understand that we have His authority and that we can use it today. *"These signs will follow those who believe: in My name **they** will cast out demons;*

they *will speak with new tongues;* *they* *will take up serpents; and if* *they* *drink anything deadly, it will by no means hurt* *them;* *they* *will lay hands on the sick, and* *they* *will recover"* (Mark 16:17–18). To whom does *"they"* refer? To those who believe and are baptized—every child of God born into the kingdom of God by the Holy Spirit. The same authority that was vested in the seventy is now vested in all who believe. Hallelujah! To cast out demons, to heal the sick, and to handle serpents as harmless things, just as Moses handled a serpent in Exodus 4:4. Moses's ministry was to deliver the people, and the ministry of Jesus was also to deliver the people, and He handed on His mantle to the church on the day of Pentecost, to continue the same ministry that the people might be delivered today. *"Let My people go"* (Exodus 9:1) is still God's cry to us today. Are we doing it, or making excuses? We have the authority and the power—all that is now required is that we should go forward and prove that it works.

> *"LET MY PEOPLE GO"* (EXODUS 9:1) IS STILL GOD'S CRY TO US TODAY. ARE WE DOING IT, OR MAKING EXCUSES? WE HAVE THE AUTHORITY AND THE POWER—ALL THAT IS NOW REQUIRED IS THAT WE SHOULD GO FORWARD AND PROVE THAT IT WORKS.

Jesus gives us a parable in Luke 11:21–22. He speaks of a strong man being armed and keeping his palace. Satan is this strong man, and he is described as the prince, or ruler, of this present world in which we live. He certainly does a good job at keeping this world bound in sin, sickness, sorrow, and suffering. But Jesus said that when a stronger man comes, he binds the strong man and delivers him of his captives and

242 The Working of Miracles and Other Prophetic Writings

takes his house and possessions. This Jesus did at Calvary, and He hands on the keys of the kingdom to all who will take them and go into Satan's strongholds to set the people free. Greater is He who is *in you* than he (Satan) who is in the world. (See 1 John 4:4.) Tremendous truths! We do not call on Jesus to do this for us; this is apologetic unbelief, for He is *in us*, and so we go forward in Him and do it *in His name*. Jesus did not tell His disciples to pray for Him to heal the sick or cast out devils— no—for we read, "*As you go,* **preach**, *saying, 'The kingdom of heaven is at hand* [present with them]. **Heal** *the sick,* **cleanse** *the lepers,* **raise** *the dead,* **cast out** *demons. Freely you have received, freely* **give**" (Matthew 10:7–8). We are on the receiving end to give to those who are in need.

As we hold on to the right hand of the Lord who got the, victory, then we take from Him the healings, deliverances, and blessings that He commands us to *give* to the people. He broke the bread and gave it to the disciples in the account of the feeding of the five thousand, but they in turn gave to the hungry. "*You give them something to eat*" (Mark 6:37) still echoes from heaven today. We do not try to be religious and kneel down and ask Him piously to do the giving for us; this is unbelief in action. We take and we give, and there will be many basketfuls left over after our ministry, so that we have a never decreasing supply to give to everyone who is hungry for God and His blessings. While we are busy giving bread, we can eat as much as we like ourselves, so both the giver and the receiver get blessed, healed, restored, and caused to prosper.

Don't limit God. This was why Israel failed to go into a land that flowed with milk and honey. They limited God. In Psalm 1, in simple language we are told that a child of God will prosper in everything that he does. This means material prosperity, mental and emotional prosperity, and spiritual prosperity. We shall have had supplied to us all things needful from the bank of heaven. This is a land that flows with milk and honey; so much milk and so much honey that we shall have twelve basketfuls left over; the cruse of God's blessings will never dry up, the barrel of meal will never cease to supply our needs. Whatsoever we do shall *prosper!* But we have to keep ourselves planted by the river of life that flows through the paradise of God. We must feed upon Him who died for us.

And so, the disciples *"went out and preached everywhere, the Lord working with them and confirming the word through the accompanying signs. Amen"* (Mark 16:20). Notice, the gospel ends with *"Amen,"* which means "so let it be." God desires that He should be given an opportunity to do His part by confirming His Word that is preached by us. These signs will be the casting out of demons, the healing of the sick, and the taking dominion over every evil sin and sickness and handling them as dead serpents and scorpions. We preach, and the signs will follow. Amen.

5

JOINT HEIRS

Now we consider the amazing teachings of the apostle Paul in his famous eighth chapter of Romans. If nothing that has been written so far has convinced the reader of our tremendous authority in Christ over all the works of Satan, then let us turn to Paul.

> For as many as are led by the Spirit of God, these are sons of God [in Greek, huios—mature sons]. For you did not receive the spirit of bondage again to fear, but you received the Spirit of adoption by whom we cry out, "Abba, Father." The Spirit Himself bears witness with our spirit that we are children of God [in Greek, teknon—new born ones], and if children, then heirs—heirs of God and joint heirs with Christ. (Romans 8:14–17)

Paul started by telling us that as mature sons of God, we can be led of His Holy Spirit. This is quite different from being led of the wisdom of man, for being led of the Holy Spirit is the daily experience of an experienced son of God who has grown out of the milk stage to the meat stage. God expects us to be led of His Spirit, which is a continual operation of the gifts of the Spirit in our daily lives. He then proceeds by explaining that if we have fear, we did not get it from God. It is an evil spirit—a demon—sent of Satan, but not of God.

What God gives us is the Holy Spirit, who adopts us into His family. As a natural born child and a legally adopted child in a family would carry the same name, the same privileges, the same standards of living, the same education, and finally would share in the estate of the father, in like manner, we are adopted into the family of God. Jesus becomes our Elder Brother, and He is the only begotten of the Father. He was conceived of the Holy Spirit, but born of a woman. He was the natural born. We are the supernatural born. He was (and is) the only begotten. We are adopted sons. We are born a second time into the kingdom of God, or family of God, by the Holy Spirit. But although He is the only begotten of God, and we are adopted out of every tongue, tribe and race on earth, we still become sons of God and are reckoned to have all the privileges, all the favors, all the blessings that belong by legal right to the Son of God. He does not withhold anything from those that walk uprightly. He is more anxious to bestow His favors: upon us than we are to receive them.

We cannot imagine or understand such blessings, such prosperity, and such health. We are as one in a dream, but the Word of God is true, *"if children, then heirs—heirs of God"* (Romans 8:17). As Jesus became the rightful possessor of all His Father's estate, so also do we become heirs of this estate through faith in Christ. We become heirs of the same estate that was given to Jesus because He was obedient unto the death of the cross. He paid for all these blessings in His own blood. They are His and they are ours.

Does He share them with us? No! They are just as much ours as His. Now we find we have become *joint heirs* with Christ. A joint heir is one who has as much right to the estate as the other joint heir. Now notice that it does not matter how many children apply for the blessing of this New Testament estate, for the *riches in glory* never dry up, and to borrow from John Bunyan's *The Pilgrim's Progress*, "The more we give away, the more we have." There is room at the cross for you, my friend, even though millions have already come. You will never exhaust the riches of glory. They are unlimited.

Jesus has taught us that He inherited all things in heaven and in earth. All power is His, the silver, the gold, the cattle, all are His by right of inheritance, because the Testator died, thus establishing, ratifying, and probating the New Testament. All the promises of the Old and New Testaments are ours today and forever. He does not share or give us handouts; He is the Good Shepherd of the sheep, and we can go in and out and find pasture, knowing the wolf shall not touch us. He is our Brother; we are His brethren. What is His is ours, and all we have to give is ourselves, and He multiplies our station, our prosperity and makes us into kings and priests. From commoners to royalty in one re-birth; no wonder so many find it hard to appreciate such riches and such glory. It seems to take us all so many years to begin to lay hold on this prosperity; we are so used to being stupid, and fearful, and poor, that it takes a little time to realize what the expression "Riches of Grace" really means!

WE MUST BE CAREFUL NOT TO SEEK RICHES
AS AN END, BUT TO SEEK ONLY JESUS AND HIS
RIGHTEOUSNESS, AND HE WILL BECOME
OUR PROSPERITY IN SPIRIT, SOUL,
AND BODY. WE SHALL LACK NOTHING, AND
THIS IS RICHES INDEED.

Some may argue that these promises are only to make us spiritually rich, but physically poor. Let us remind you that Jesus told us He became poor to make many rich. (See 2 Corinthians 6:10.) We must be careful not to seek riches as an end, but to seek only Jesus and His righteousness, and He will become our prosperity in spirit, soul, and body. We shall lack nothing, and this is riches indeed. Let us not indulge again in apologetics, but enter into His riches in glory by Christ Jesus. John knew this when he wrote, *"Beloved, I pray that you may prosper in all things and be in health, just as your soul prospers"* (3 John 1:2).

David, in Old Testament times, put no division between the blessings of soul and body health. We have two feet to tread upon the two curses of Satan, the scorpion of sin and the serpent of sickness. *"Bless the* LORD, *O my soul, and forget not* **all** *His benefits: who forgives* **all** *your iniquities, who heals* **all** *your diseases"* (Psalm 103:2–3). His power and authority is sufficient, for if He puts all things under His feet, then they are under ours also, if we abide in Him, for our feet become His feet on earth, our hands His hands, for our bodies are the temples of the Holy Spirit through which God wishes to manifest the Son by the Holy Spirit

Before we leave this chapter, we must refer again to the apostle Paul, but this time in Galatians 4 where he gives us a double witness to the amazing truth of our adoption into the royal family of God. He begins by reminding us that we were under bondage before we found liberty in Christ, but Jesus redeemed us, or purchased us from this bondage into the glorious liberty of the sons of God. It was as if we were a slave to Satan. Jesus came and paid the price of His own blood and we were set free from the power of Satan, for *"Therefore if the Son makes you free, you shall be free indeed"* (John 8:36). Thus, a complete freedom from want, fear, poverty, suffering, and sickness was given to us as a free gift, and is called the good news of the kingdom of God. Good news indeed. One hundred percent free.

The redemption price at Calvary introduced the law of adoption. By believing with our whole hearts that Jesus paid the penalty of our sins, we were reckoned to have been adopted by God into His family. We may not have been aware of this, nor of the amazing blessings that accrue to us, but God reckoned it nevertheless, and it is as we become aware of this truth that we progressively enter into a greater degree of blessings as we exercise our faith, and our faith only comes through reading and believing the Word of God. Paul concluded therefore, by telling us that we are no more servants, but *sons*, and if a son, then an heir of God through Christ. It is all through our Elder Brother.

Are you *free indeed?*

6

IN HEAVENLY PLACES

In chapter one, we wrote on the creation of man, how God created them, male and female in His likeness, and that they were a little lower than the angels.

Now notice the tremendous change that takes place when Jesus incorporates us into His royal family. No longer a little below the angels, but now lifted up into heavenly places in *Christ*. (See Ephesians 2:6.) It is always necessary to remember that as we abide *in Christ*, we are where He is. He is the New Creation, and we also are reckoned to be a new creation in *Him*. If He is far above all principality and power, might, and dominion, and every name that is named, not only in this world, but also that which is to come (see Ephesians 1:21), then we also are positionally the same when we learn to abide in Him. No wonder Jesus told His disciples that they had power over all the power of Satan. Only Jesus obtained that power through the cross, and now we are joint heirs with Him in His reigning position on the right hand of God, set down in heavenly places. This truth is so amazing, that it alarms the timid who think more of their unworthiness than His worthiness. *"Worthy is the Lamb"* (Revelation 5:12), the angels cried.

Paul understood this truth when he reminded us that *"we do not wrestle against flesh and blood, but against principalities, against powers, against the rulers of the darkness of this age, against spiritual hosts of wickedness in the heavenly places"* (Ephesians 6:12). In this verse are enumerated the various degrees of Satanic spiritual wickedness. These are not earthly powers; they are Satanic spiritual powers that control earthly kingdoms, dictatorships, political systems, and religious systems opposed to God. Every evil foul demon working for Satan is mentioned in the categories; Paul said we wrestle with them!

Is this a hopeless wrestling match? Are the odds 100-to-1 against us? Do we go in the ring doomed to be pulverized by these powers? No, a thousand times no. We go in to win, to defeat the enemy by commanding, by prayer, by our very attitude of victory. The very moment Satan sees us enter the wrestling ring, he knows that he is defeated before we start. He will certainly put up stiff and stubborn opposition, but he knows he is defeated, and it is only a matter of time before he will throw in the towel and declare that he can no longer oppress us in the way he tried so hard to do. Our faith must *never waiver*. The battle may be long and fierce, but *"I can do all things through Christ who strengthens me"* (Philippians 4:13). Defeat is not in the dictionary of heaven unless it speaks of Satan and his demons. For the Christian, there is only victory all the time.

Why is this? It is because our lives are hid in Christ in God, and the wicked one touches us not. Resist the devil and he will flee from you.

When ministering in Uruapan, Mexico, we met a Christian man who was a cotton grower with a farm given to him by the Mexican government. The surrounding cotton farmers resented his faith, for they were fanatical religionists being stirred up by their priests. They commanded this man to leave his farm, and he refused. They came again and ordered him to run and they would shoot him. He refused to run and told them he would stay where God had put him. Then an enraged fanatic said he would shoot him where he stood, so he said, "Go ahead and shoot, but I'm not quitting," at which a strange thing happened; the man began to tremble violently and he turned and slunk away. This is a true story, for the man gave me his sombrero as a memento of a New Testament story. Resist the devil steadfastly *in the faith*. Sometimes we do not wrestle long enough. We give up and *Satan wins*, whereas he was only supposed to lose and run!

BEFORE CALVARY, MAN HAD BEEN CREATED IN GOD'S LIKENESS, BUT A LITTLE LOWER THAN THE ANGELS, INCLUDING MICHAEL THE ARCHANGEL, BUT AFTER CALVARY WE WERE ELEVATED FAR ABOVE ALL PRINCIPALITIES AND POWERS.

We once had an objection raised to this teaching of our authority in Christ. How could we command Satan when even the great and mighty archangel Michael dare not rebuke Satan himself, but said, "*The Lord rebuke you!*" (Jude 1:9)? This is a wonderful and marvelous revelation. Before Calvary, man had been created in God's likeness, but a little lower than the angels, including Michael the archangel, but after Calvary we were elevated far above all principalities and powers. Now an angel becomes a ministering spirit to those who are heirs of this salvation. This is where our position of being joint heirs with Christ is rightly understood. Now Michael and other angels become our ministering spirits; now we are recreated *in Christ* to be above them, not a little lower, but now far above. As Michael never sinned, he was never lost, and so does not need a Savior. It was the fallen angels who sinned, and were divested of their spiritual bodies and position. They were cast out into the earth (see Revelation 12:9–10), but Michael is still an archangel and is still subject to obedience of rank. Satan was created the greatest and the most powerful of all the angels, and Michael was next in rank with others like Gabriel, therefore Michael could not rebuke his superior officer, even if his superior officer had sinned. He still carries his rank, for the callings of God are not to be repented of. He now uses this rank to break down God's heritage instead of helping to build it up by ministering to it, as Michael does.

Satan was created as the supreme commander-in-chief of all angelic forces. Before the cross, he even entered heaven to give an account of himself, as we read in Job 1 and 2, and he correctly reported that he was walking to and fro in the earth, for that was his domain, as prince of this world. At the cross, Satan fell heavily again and lost his right of entry into heaven, but he never lost his rank. (See Luke 10:18.) Michael cannot rebuke Satan, but Jesus did, so we can do so today in His name. This is why we cast out demons in the name of Jesus; we heal the sick in the name of Jesus; we can do all things in the name of Jesus, even commanding a mountain to be cast into the sea, and if we do not doubt in our hearts, it will happen! Try it and see! We suggest we begin with mountains of difficulties before we join forces with the earthmovers!

Thus we find in God's Word that He is imploring us to understand our high calling in Christ.

> *That the God of our Lord Jesus Christ,...may give to you the spirit of wisdom and revelation in the **knowledge of Him**, the eyes of your understanding being enlightened; that you may know what is the hope of His calling, what are the riches of the glory of His inheritance in the saints, and what is the exceeding greatness of His power toward us **who believe**, according to the working of His mighty power which He worked in Christ when He raised Him from the dead and seated Him at His right hand in the heavenly places, far above all principality...power...might...dominion...name.... And He put all things under His feet.* (Ephesians 1:17–22)

This is the position of Jesus Christ today. God put Him there after He raised Him from the dead, and as we abide in Him, and are *"found in Him"* (Philippians 3:9) we can exercise all the power and authority that He vests in us, His brethren and sisters.

In Romans 8:11, Paul recorded that *"if the Spirit of Him who raised Jesus from the dead dwells in you, He who raised Christ from the dead will also give life to your mortal bodies through His Spirit who dwells in you"* (Romans 8:11). The quickening power of the Holy Spirit will be continually restoring our mortal body to health and strength for every time of need in our victorious battle against Satan. Finally, when it is God's time (and not Satan's time) for us to go to be with the Lord, He will quicken our bodies so completely that we will have a body which is from heaven. (See 2 Corinthians 5:1–2.) Every punch that Satan might put into us, in suffering, sickness, frustration, and sorrow, if resisted, will be repulsed by the quickening power of the Spirit of God in our mortal bodies. Perhaps this is what Paul had in mind when he wrote that if a believer speaks in tongues he edifies himself, for in so doing, he would cause the Spirit of God to move mightily in his mortal body. Paul also recommended to Timothy that he stir up the gift that was in him. Christians today have been far more prone to let the devil stir them up and kick them around, and stamp on them, rather than taking the initiative and stirring up the Holy Spirit in them, going into Satan like a quarterback and knocking him down and casting him out of the way. It may seem a crude thing to say, but either Satan is going to kick you around, or you are going to kick him around. Just choose which position you want to play on this winning team!

7

MIGHTY TO THE PULLING DOWN OF STRONGHOLDS

Not only did Paul tell us we were more than conquerors through Christ, but he also taught us that we are *mighty* to the pulling down of strongholds. (See 2 Corinthians 10:4.) This means that in Christ, we are a mighty breed, mighty men and women, strong and invincible; in fact, like David, we can tear in pieces the lion and the bear that attack the sheep of God. How wonderful if every pastor could realize this. When the devil comes like a roaring lion into your assembly, or comes like a strong bear, you are *mighty* to pull the lion and the bear to bits and destroy them before they destroy you or the flock over which God has made you the overseer.

Mighty to the pulling down. Every high and exalted thing that rears its ugly head against Christ and His church is your prey to pull down. It matters not how strong or tall, or how loud the roaring, you are *mighty* to tear it down. It may have taken a week, but Joshua was *mighty* to the pulling down of the stronghold of Jericho. Moses was *mighty* to divide the Red Sea; Caleb was *mighty* to take a mountain; Samson was *mighty* to pull down a house over his head. This *mighty* army of conquering heroes is mentioned in Hebrews 11, and in verses 33–34 it is recorded: "*Who **through faith** subdued kingdoms, worked righteousness, obtained promises, stopped the mouths of lions, quenched the violence of fire, escaped the edge of the sword, out of weakness were made **strong**, became valiant in battle, turned to flight the armies of the aliens.*" Mighty men of valor.

Gideon reacted as we might when suddenly God said to him, "*The* LORD *is with you, you mighty man of valor!*" (Judges 6:12). Gideon agreed to obey God and was used to deliver Israel. He could have refused, but God reckoned him to be a mighty man of valor nevertheless. God looks on each one of us as *mighty* men and women of valor as we abide in His Son. Every one of us is *mighty* in Christ to pull down the opposing forces of Satan arrayed against us so formidably. These forces are arrayed against the church, which is so weak and feeble, when God reckons it to be so strong and mighty. These forces are arrayed against us in our homes and private lives; they affect our spiritual and physical health; we are oppressed and give way instead of resisting and pulling down.

In every major city of the world today, there are gaps where old buildings are being pulled down to make way for new ones to be built. The machines used seem to be mighty to the pulling down of well-entrenched buildings, and we are glad to see bright new buildings take their place. The pulling down has to take place before the new creation. All around us we see things that need to be pulled down before God can build a new life, a new home, or new church.

This principle is brought out in Jeremiah 1:7–9. First, God told Jeremiah to speak only what He told him, and that He would be responsible for putting words in his mouth. He was not to be afraid of anyone, however demon-possessed they appeared to be, or however politically strong, for God promised to be *with him* to deliver him. God can deliver us only if we do what He commands. Let us not be like Jonah and run away! First, Jeremiah had to *root out*; second, *pull down*; third, *destroy*; fourth, *throw down*. These four necessary things were to utterly destroy and remove all the works of Satan in Israel. Even right down to the basements of Satan's works, Jeremiah was to root out the last remains of evil. Then when the ground was cleared—after he had been *mighty* to pull down the strongholds—he was to *build* and to *plant*. We find that Jesus did all this perfectly. He destroyed the old order and brought in the New Testament building of God, built of lively stones, without the help of man.

The Old Testament temple typified the new, but much of Israel clung to its old religion, so God caused Titus, the Roman general, to come down in AD 70 and destroy the city and the temple, which fulfilled Daniel 9:26. The Jews had these prophecies in their scrolls, but failed to recognize their Savior and Messiah when He came. On the cross, our Savior utterly pulled down and destroyed all the works of Satan. It is for us today to use our vested authority and do the same, remembering that God is with us, and will deliver us, even as He did Jeremiah.

GOD ONLY SEES US AS MIGHTY MEN AND WOMEN OF VALOR. WE SOMETIMES SEE OURSELVES AS CRAVEN DEFEATED UNWORTHY CHILDREN OF GOD.

Friends, we *are mighty*. God only sees us as mighty men and women of valor. We sometimes see ourselves as craven defeated unworthy children of God. The idea seems to be, "Satan, if you leave us alone, we will leave you alone." Let us make a pact of peaceful coexistence with Satan. We will give him room if he gives us room. We will compromise and learn to live together. Is this your philosophy my friend? God's Word says, "Go in, defeat him, tear him down, spoil his goods, throw him out, and then build on his territory the kingdom of God with saved lives, delivered human living stones for the New Testament temple." *"Every place that the sole of your foot will tread upon I have given you"* (Joshua 1:3).

Not only are we *mighty* to the pulling down of strongholds of Satan, but we are *mighty* to remove the rubble of false teaching, apologetics, and weaknesses. Jesus made this clear by telling us to have the faith of God, and then with this gift of faith, we could cast the mountain into the sea if we doubted not in our hearts. Long ago, Zerubbabel, when building the temple under much persecution and provocation, commanded *"Who are you O great mountain? Before Zerubbabel you shall become a plain!"* (Zechariah 4:7). Our *mightiness* is not by natural strength of armies or munitions nor by national power, but by the *Spirit of God.* It is this anointing that *breaks* the yoke of Satan, and pulls down his strongholds. It is this great baptism of the Spirit, which He gives to all who ask Him, that gives us this tremendous dynamic power to attack, tear down, break, and subdue the works of Satan. The church has for so long relied on politics, doctrines, bylaws, and committees that it has forgotten to rely on the Holy Spirit alone. The church is supposed to be terrible as an army with banners, a winning army.

This state will not continue. We are now in the time of great revival, the return of the power of God to the church. Multitudes in all denominations are being baptized afresh in the Holy Spirit; a new vision is being seen; a new day is dawning. *"When the enemy comes in like a flood, the* **Spirit** *of the* LORD *will lift up a standard against him"* (Isaiah 59:19). We shall become a terrible army with banners; we shall hear the voice of the Lord coming to us in the gifts of the Spirit in our churches, the precious charismatic gifts which He is giving back to us, *"The* LORD *gives voice before His army, for His camp is very great; for strong is the One who executes His word"* (Joel 2:11).

We believe that this little book will play its part in awakening God's people to realize what giants He has made us, and that the tide of evil has reached its high water mark; it is now time for God to blow with His spiritual wind of the Spirit, through His church, to blow back this tide of evil and set the people free. All over the world, nations have received their independence. Africa is wide open to Christ or chaos, which shall it be? South America is seething to bring forth a new order. What shall this new order be, Christ or socialism? Asia is wrestling with destiny. Which way will she go? We have the answer. We are God's people, *mighty* to the pulling down of these ancient strongholds of Satan. Our prayers must be the strong believing prayers of faith, our praises full of faith and joy. If we doubt not in our hearts, Jesus said, we shall have whatsoever *we say* and *command*. God will not let the world go to the devil or continue to be ruled by antichrists, as long as Jesus is on the right hand of God and we are complete in Him. We must arise now, and force Satan to give ground by sending the gospel—the full gospel with signs following—to every nation, by evangelist, by literature, by radio.

Let us arise in a newness of faith, buckle on the gospel armor, take up the sword of the Spirit and the shield of faith, and pull down the strongholds of Satan. This is God's hour, and our opportunity. *We are mighty in Him.*

8

WHO ARE WE?

The greatest hindrance to the realization of our tremendous power and authority as Christians is Satan's lie that "we are not worthy." This produces a powerful inferiority complex and freezes us into a state of spiritual immobility. It is the age-old stratagem of Satan to say, *"Has God indeed said…?"* (Genesis 3:1). Yes, He has said it! We are powerful, we are invincible, we are more than conquerors, we have all the winning weapons; if we fight according to His rules *we cannot lose. It is impossible to lose.*

Who are we? We are *sons of God*, and we are worthy in Him. We repudiate utterly the old lie heard in so many defeated churches that "we are not worthy." What does Jesus say? When He wrote to the church in Sardis, a typical Christian church that exists in our cities today, He said that there were some in Sardis *who were worthy*, and they would walk with Him in white. (See Revelation 3:4.) The reward of walking in white was given solely on the grounds that they *were worthy* because they did not defile themselves. Presumably, the other Christians at Sardis would walk in gray, or some other color, and they were not worthy. It is this second class of Christian who is always in trouble and always excusing himself for his troubles, by comparing himself with other "gray Christians" and then postulating the theory that it is normal Christianity to be defeated, to be sick, to be depressed and to be on the losing side most of the time. The "white Christians" know who they are. They do not apologize for God's Word; they believe it and live it, and their lives are blessed to themselves and to all others with whom they come in contact. They do not go down in defeat, for they will not defile themselves with Satan or his works of darkness. They walk in the light as Jesus is in the light. They do not compromise, they resist the devil steadfastly in the faith, and this becomes their normal Christian experience. There is nothing abnormal about continual victory. It is the normal Christian life. Anything less is abnormal or subnormal.

They walk in white for they are worthy.

Yes, we are sons of God, co-heirs of Christ, possessors of all His riches in glory as our inheritance. (See Ephesians 1:18.) All the power, strength, might, health, and prosperity sufficient for our needs, is ours now. Co-heirs with our elder Brother, *the only begotten Son* of God. Let us hold our heads high. Let us know our calling and our authority, and, with love and determination, pull down the works and lies of Satan wherever we find them. This book is dedicated to that end.

Who are we? We are kings and priests. (See Revelation 1:6.) There are some who insist that this Scripture should read, "We are a kingdom of priests." We will not quarrel with this, but the literal Greek tells us we are kings as well as priests. This has a clear meaning. We therefore are divine royalty; our blood has been cleansed by His precious blood and now royal blood is in our veins, carrying the power of the Holy Spirit in every corpuscle.

There is no need to tell Prince Charles that he is of royal blood. He knows it, for his mother is queen. Does God have to remind us that we are royal also, for our Father is God and our Brother is King of Kings and Lord of Lords? Not by right of birth, but by right of adoption, cleansing and sanctification. Notice the wording of Revelation 1:5–6: *"Jesus Christ...has made us **kings and priests**."* He did this by washing us in His own blood! We realize that it is very hard for humble people born in humble circumstances to realize that Jesus Christ turns them into a king or a queen, but Scripture teaches it, and those who begin to ask Jesus to give them grace and ability to walk as kings and queens find that He does so. One of the fundamental teachings of royalty is that they are always gracious and never make those of lesser station in life feel uncomfortable.

We are also *priests*. Peter taught us that we should offer spiritual sacrifices as priests. We should pray and intercede for others; we should plead the precious blood on their behalf, for the Old Testament priest used to sprinkle blood every day, and so should we—the blood of Jesus. We should offer the sacrifice of praise continually for all His wonderful blessings, not just sometimes, but continually. We should give of our time and talents to Jesus, a tithe of our time, talents and money, and offerings afterward.

Who are we? A chosen generation—regenerated by the Holy Spirit, born again into His kingdom, born to be priests and kings. Chosen and called of God for a high office. A peculiar people; that is, unusual, out of the normal run, regenerate, different; and it must be obvious to all that we are different; not fanatically different, but radiantly different, diffusing the love and graces of God in every breath and look. Having His power and authority. A peculiar people indeed!

GOD WILL SHOW US THE STRATAGEMS OF SATAN, AND THEN WE CAN BEGIN TO TAKE OUR ABSOLUTE AUTHORITY OVER HIM AND ALL HIS WORKS OF SIN AND SICKNESS, NOT ONLY FOR OURSELVES BUT FOR OTHERS ALSO.

Never again say, "I can't." For it is written, "*I can **do all things** through Christ who strengthens me*" (Philippians 4:13). There is not one thing you cannot do. You are "the boss." Satan is "the slave."

Satan is very subtle, and he will very easily deceive us, unless we wait on the Lord with the gift of discerning of spirits, and other charismatic gifts He gives to those who are filled with His Spirit. God will show us the stratagems of Satan, and then we can begin to take our absolute authority over him and all his works of sin and sickness, not only for ourselves but for others also.

More than conquerors and mighty to the pulling down of strong-holds—that is who we are!

ADDENDUM

This book is purposely written in a very positive tone to help make people realize their tremendous power and authority as sons of God. There may be some who will say, "What about the Scripture '*If we suffer, we shall also reign with him*' (2 Timothy 2:12 KJV)"? Is not suffering in God's plan? Yes it is, truly, but if you wish to identify yourself with Christ's sufferings, do not include sickness, for He was never sick. He was a Man of Sorrows, acquainted with grief; He was persecuted, spat upon, insulted, and He asked His disciples if they were willing to be baptized with the baptism of His sufferings, and they said they were; and indeed, they did suffer with Him. Remember, in Psalm 34:19, that though the sufferings of the Christians are many, yet the Lord *delivers* him out of them *all*! Satan will attack, and God will use his attacks to purify and make us more like Himself, but do not wallow in the suffering. Jesus died to redeem us from these things; claim the promises of God and rise out of every battle victorious.

Christianity is not a rest cure. It is not a bed of roses, but a battle to the finish against the world, the flesh, and the devil, but in this protracted battle, God expects us to win every round! When we slip, we rise and fight on. In the description of the warrior-Christian in Ephesians 6, we are told that having done all, we are to stand and withstand. *No* falling down or being knocked down!

Thanks be to God, who gives us the victory through our Lord Jesus Christ. (1 Corinthians 15:57)

ABOUT THE AUTHOR

The picture of a British bulldog, H. A. Maxwell Whyte (1908–1988) had a commanding countenance and a stentorian voice, which was especially awesome when raised against the devil and his demons. He had a big, soft heart, and he loved Jesus. He was a pioneer in this generation in recognizing that *"we do not wrestle against flesh and blood, but against principalities, against powers, against the rulers of the darkness of this age, against spiritual hosts of wickedness in the heavenly places"* (Ephesians 6:12), and he has carried the battle right to the enemy's doorstep. He had faith enough to believe that God would confirm His *"word through the accompanying signs"* (Mark 16:20). In the powerful name of Jesus, he has proclaimed liberty to the captives and opened the prisons for those who were bound. (See Isaiah 61:1.) For more than forty years, he ministered worldwide to the downcast and brokenhearted and led the way in the ministry of the powerful gifts of the Holy Spirit.

Maxwell Whyte was born on May 3, 1908, in London, England. As a child, he was raised in a nominally Christian home in which church attendance was encouraged. Raised as a Presbyterian, Maxwell was strongly influenced by the godly pastor of his boyhood parish, and at age sixteen, he made a commitment to the Lord, although his level of understanding of what this decision meant was meager indeed.

After completing his education at Dulwich College in London, Maxwell entered the business world as a representative of the Anglo-American Oil Company, and even during the Depression years, he enjoyed a measure of success that was the envy of many during those years of economic stress. On June 8, 1934, Maxwell married Olive Hughes in St. Paul's Anglican Church in the London suburb of Beckenham. It was in this peaceful residential area that Maxwell and Olive rejoiced in their comfortable lifestyle, their solid marriage, and the birth of their first two sons, David and Michael.

All was going well for this successful and happy couple until son David became seriously ill. In fear that their son might be taken from them, Olive and Maxwell cried out to the Lord in desperation, and they were both dramatically affected when God restored David to good health. Shortly after this experience, Maxwell was invited by a colleague to attend a small charismatic meeting in Croydon on the outskirts of London. There, for the first time, he witnessed the operation of the gifts of the Holy Spirit and saw a group of people whose relationship with the Lord was one of vitality, not in keeping with religious tradition. Maxwell's life was never the same again as he was truly converted, baptized in water, baptized in the Holy Spirit, and miraculously set free from a smoking habit, all within a few weeks. The year was 1939, and to be a charismatic in those days was not a popular thing for a Christian to be!

At the outbreak of World War II, Maxwell entered the Royal Air Force as a signals officer, where his lifelong interest in amateur radio was put to use in setting up defense communications. During his six and a half years of military service, Maxwell spent many long hours studying the Bible, convinced that one day he would enter into full-time ministry. In 1946, after his discharge from the RAF, Maxwell returned to his business career, only to leave it a few months later to prepare for the ministry. After several months of intensive training and prayer, Maxwell answered the call to emigrate to Toronto, Canada, to be pastor of the United Apostolic Faith Church, a small congregation that had been without a pastor for several years.

So it was, in April 1947, that Maxwell and Olive Whyte and their family of three boys (Stephen was born a few months after the war) arrived in Canada to take up the responsibility of leading a group of a dozen or so believers who made up the fledgling congregation in Toronto. The first few years in Toronto were not easy for the Whytes. They lived in cramped quarters on little income, and in 1952, a fourth son, John, was born. The boys adjusted well to their new environment and soon became full-fledged Canadians. For over three decades, Maxwell faithfully served as pastor to this church. He witnessed the transformation of the small band of worshippers as God built them into a thriving group of believers who held to the charismatic truths of the Bible.

In 1948, while Maxwell was dealing with one of his parishioners who suffered from chronic asthma and another who was suicidal, God sovereignly directed him into an understanding of the reality of spiritual warfare and deliverance. This revelation catapulted Maxwell into a ministry that drew attention from many parts of the globe.

In over forty years of ministry, Whyte ministered in many countries of the world on five continents. At the same time, he authored numerous books dealing with the workings of God in the present charismatic outpourings of the Spirit. Hundreds of letters have told of healings and deliverances of those who have read his writings, believed, and were blessed.